PREVENTION AND CONSULTATION

Other Books in the Prevention Practice Kit

Program Development and Evaluation in Prevention (9781452258010)

Prevention Groups (9781452257983)

Prevention in Psychology (9781452257952)

Social Justice and Culturally Relevant Prevention (9781452257969)

Public Policy and Mental Health (9781452258027)

Evidence-Based Prevention (9781452258003)

Best Practices in Prevention (9781452257976)

Dedicated with love to my wife Leslie and our children Matt and Ashley

PREVENTION AND CONSULTATION

A. MICHAEL DOUGHERTY

Western Carolina University

Los Angeles | London | New Delhi
Singapore | Washington DC

Los Angeles | London | New Delhi
Singapore | Washington DC

FOR INFORMATION:

SAGE Publications, Inc.
2455 Teller Road
Thousand Oaks, California 91320
E-mail: order@sagepub.com

SAGE Publications Ltd.
1 Oliver's Yard
55 City Road
London EC1Y 1SP
United Kingdom

SAGE Publications India Pvt. Ltd.
B 1/I 1 Mohan Cooperative Industrial Area
Mathura Road, New Delhi 110 044
India

SAGE Publications Asia-Pacific Pte. Ltd.
3 Church Street
#10-04 Samsung Hub
Singapore 049483

Acquisitions Editor: Kassie Graves
Editorial Assistant: Elizabeth Luizzi
Production Editor: Brittany Bauhaus
Copy Editor: QuADS Prepress (P) Ltd.
Typesetter: C&M Digitals (P) Ltd.
Proofreader: Jeff Bryant
Indexer: Diggs Publication Services, Inc.
Cover Designer: Glenn Vogel
Marketing Manager: Lisa Sheldon Brown
Permissions Editor: Adele Hutchinson

Copyright © 2013 by SAGE Publications, Inc.

Printed in the United States of America

Library of Congress Cataloging-in-Publication Data

Prevention and consultation / editors, A. Michael Dougherty.

p. cm. — (Prevention practice kit)
Includes bibliographical references and index.

ISBN 978-1-4522-5799-0 (pbk.)

1. Preventive health services. 2. Psychological consultation. I. Dougherty, A. Michael, 1945-

RA427.P7374 2013
158.3—dc23   2012040374

This book is printed on acid-free paper.

12 13 14 15 16 10 9 8 7 6 5 4 3 2 1

Brief Contents _____

Detailed Contents _____

Acknowledgments_____

I acknowledge the impact that the students I have taught over the past three and a half decades at Western Carolina University have had on my thinking about consultation and its many variations, including prevention.

1

Introduction to Consultation

The purpose of this volume is twofold. First, I provide a summary review of the literature on consultation as a service provided by mental health/human service professionals. Second, I review the literature on the preventive aspects of consultation and provide related examples and case studies. My main goal is to present the reader with information and examples for use in becoming even more engaged in prevention activities and practice.

The Nature of Consultation

Consultation is an indirect service frequently provided by psychologists, counselors, social workers, and other mental health/human service professionals in a variety of settings (Dougherty, 2009a). Consultation can be defined as "a process in which a human service professional assists a consultee with a work-related (or caretaking-related) problem with a client system, with the goal of helping both the consultee and client system in some specified way" (Dougherty, 2009a, p. 4). As Conyne (2004) notes, "The consultant (Point 'A') works through others (Point 'B') to benefit a third party (Point 'C')" (p. 77). Consultees tend to be one or more mental health/human service professionals, other professionals with a direct role with the client system, or caregivers such as parents. The client system can be an individual, a group, an organization, or even an entire community.

Consultation has several characteristics that, when taken together, differentiate it from other services such as counseling/psychotherapy, supervision, teaching, and mediation. First, consultation typically uses a *problem-solving process*. Problem solving is a process that involves identifying, defining, and finding a solution to a problem. Second, consultation is *tripartite*, the three parties being the consultant, the consultee, and the client system. Third, consultation is an *indirect service* in that the consultant does not work directly with the client system. Rather, the consultant provides direct service to the consultee who, in turn, provides direct service to the client system. Thus, the consultant provides indirect service to the client system through the intermediary of the consultee.

1

Historically, several authors, for example Caplan (1970) and Gutkin and Curtis (1999), have suggested other commonly accepted characteristics of consultation:

- Participation is voluntary for all parties.
- Consultees are under no obligation to follow the consultant's recommendations.
- The relationship between the consultant and the consultee is between equals.
- Consultation deals with work-related (or caregiving-related) problems and avoids dealing with the personal issues of consultees.
- Either the consultee or the client system can be the primary focus of change depending on the nature of the consultation.
- Consultation can be a stand-alone service or be part of a broader program.
- Consultation tends to be both remedial and preventive in that the current client system is helped, and the consultee is able to effectively work with similar situations in the future.

The Skill Sets and Roles of Consultants

What skill sets are needed for effective consultation? Interpersonal and communication skills form the foundation for the consultant's activity. Because the cultural context of consultation influences its delivery, consultants should possess a strong set of multicultural skills. Consultation itself is a problem-solving process. Clearly, a strong set of problem-solving skills is essential for the consultant. The organizational context in which consultation occurs can affect the process and can be a target of change. Consequently, a skill set in working with organizations is essential for consultants. Consultants are increasingly being asked to work with groups of consultees. This trend dictates that consultants need to be able to effectively work with groups of consultees in several ways. Finally, and obviously, consultants need the professional and ethical skills to be able to act in a professional manner during the consultation relationship.

Consultants can take on a variety of roles when they consult. The role(s) that consultants engage in are a function of several variables, including the skills, orientation, and values of the consultant and the consultee, and the nature of the problem being dealt with. Common roles assumed by consultants have been delineated by Lippitt and Lippitt (1986). These roles are typically placed on a continuum from directive to nondirective. These roles include advocate, expert, trainer/educator, collaborator, fact finder, and process specialist.

Advocacy is the most directive role and occurs when the consultant uses persuasion to influence a consultee's decision regarding action with the client system. Consultants also engage in this role when they are promoting social justice. The expert role is traditionally the most frequently taken on role by consultants and includes some form of specialized knowledge, recommendations, or service that the consultant provides. When engaging in the trainer/educator role, the consultant works with the consultee to acquire new knowledge and/or skills for use with the client system. In the collaborator role, the consultant and the consultee pool their respective resources to assist the consultee in determining a course of action for him or her to follow while working with the client system. As we will see, the collaborator role can effectively promote prevention through actively engaging the consultee in all aspects of the consultation process. It is the opinion of this author that consultants utilize the collaborative role to the extent possible when consulting. As a fact finder, the consultant engages in information gathering and then provides that information in an organized manner to the consultee to make use of it when working with the client system. The process specialist is the least directive role and the consultant focuses on process issues (*how* things are being done) rather than on content issues (*what* is being done).

Learning Exercise 1

You Are on a "Role"

You have just been introduced to some of the roles consultants can take in their work. Based on what you know right now, rank order these roles in terms of how comfortable you would be in engaging in them (1 = *most comfortable*; 6 = *least comfortable*).

_____ advocate

_____ expert

_____ trainer/educator

_____ collaborator

_____ fact finder

_____ process specialist

The Consultation Process

There are typically five aspects to the consultation process. These include relationship building, problem identification, problem analysis, intervention implementation, and program evaluation (Frank & Kratochwill, 2008). Dougherty (2009b) has incorporated these aspects into a four-stage generic model of consultation. This model, dynamic in nature, provides a framework that psychologists, counselors, and other mental health/human service professionals can employ when providing consultation.

The first stage is the entry stage. This stage consists of four phases: (1) exploring organizational needs, (2) contracting, (3) physically entering the system, and (4) psychologically entering the system. During this stage, the consultant attends to relationship building, obtains a grasp on the problem to be dealt with, sets up a physical presence, and moves to acceptance by the consultee.

Diagnosis, Stage 2, typically involves data gathering, problem identification, goal setting, and the generation of possible interventions. In this stage, the consultant and the consultee work together to determine what the actual problem is. Together, they target the nature and direction of changes to be made in the client system and brainstorm possible interventions that may work.

The third stage is referred to as the implementation stage. The stage includes the phases of choosing an intervention, developing a plan, implementing the plan, and evaluating the plan. This stage tends to be the longest in the consultation process and is often the most complex. In this stage, the consultant is "on call" while the consultee implements the intervention.

The final stage is disengagement. During this stage, the four phases of (1) evaluating the consultation process, (2) planning postconsultation matters, (3) reducing involvement and following up, and (4) terminating the consultative relationship are completed. Table 1.1 summarizes the stages of consultation.

Table 1.1   The Stages of Consultation

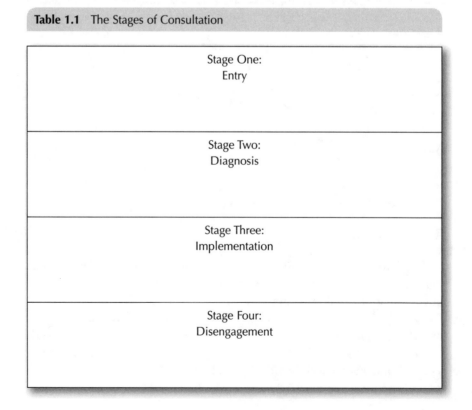

Stage One: Entry
Stage Two: Diagnosis
Stage Three: Implementation
Stage Four: Disengagement

It is important to remember that in real life, this model is dynamic with the stages often overlapping. For example, if the consultant and consultee err in the initial definition of the problem, the process may revert back to that phase again when the implementation fails to meet the established criteria of the goal-setting process.

Limitations of Consultation

Consultation is not without its limitations. First, consultation is just one service that mental health professionals can provide. It is not a panacea and may not be the best course of action to take, given the situation being dealt with even when prevention is a goal (Caplan, 1970; Dougherty, 2009b). Second, as we shall see later on in this text, consultation is not well researched. Its practice has far outpaced its research base (Erchul & Sheridan, 2008). As a result, practitioners need to be cautious in assuming that the actions they take in consultation have strong empirical evidence to back them up. Third, there is a limited albeit growing knowledge base regarding the multicultural aspects of consultation and how they inform its practice (Ingraham, 2004, 2008). Finally, the complexity of consultation makes it likely that practitioners will encounter complex ethical issues in its practice (Dougherty, 2009b). For example, confidentiality takes on an added dimension.

2 Background Theory on Consultation

The emergence of consultation as a service option for mental health/ human service professionals was due to many reasons. First, there was the issue, pointed out by authors such as Albee (1959), of the increasing incidence of mental health problems in our society with a corresponding shortage of mental health professionals to help deal with these problems. Second, the emergence of preventive psychiatry with its focus on population-based perspectives (Caplan, 1964) became popular. The idea behind this was the following: Rather than deal exclusively with remedial issues, psychiatry had the capacity to make preventive interventions in the community that would decrease the occurrence of mental health issues among the populace. By being involved in social forces that impact the occurrence of psychological problems, both negatively and positively, preventive programs can be developed to reduce the incidence of mental illness. Such outcomes would be based on psychiatry dealing with community dynamics and delivering interventions related to program planning, program staff competence, and program evaluation. Hence, psychiatry would have a preventive effect that promoted the psychological well-being of the community and simultaneously reduced the incidence of mental health problems in the community. Third, alternative therapies to those related to the psychodynamic model emerged, and their use as a framework for consultation provided broader approaches for the use of consultation concepts. Fourth, legislation, the Community Mental Health Centers Act of 1963, P. L. 88-164, included consultation as an authorized service (Zins, 1995).

Models of Consultation

Although there are several models of consultation, three particular models have emerged as the most popular, and they can be used in any setting. These are (1) behavioral, (2) mental health, and (3) organizational consultation (Dougherty, 2009b). There are most likely more similarities than differences among these models. Differences tend to be more related to the theoretical perspective on consultation itself rather than on its processes.

Behavioral Consultation

Bergan (1977), a pioneer in the behavioral consultation movement, reported two theoretical influences on behavioral consultation: system theory as it relates to problem solving (e.g., Kaufman, 1971) and behavioral psychology (e.g., Bandura, 1969). Systems theory in terms of problem solving describes the problem-solving process as a series of discrete steps. Feedback is used to assist the problem-solving process to achieve a solution to the defined problem (Bergan, 1977; Bergan & Kratochwill, 1990). In terms of the influence of behavioral psychology, the behavioral consultation model originally leaned heavily on Skinnerian operant conditioning principles and learning theory. Application of the developments in behavioral therapy over the years expanded the scope of behavioral consultation to include the influence of all areas of learning theory. Bandura's (1977) social learning theory, the Pavlovian model of classical conditioning, cognitive behavior modification (Meichenbaum, 1977), and behavioral ecology (Willems, 1974) have created opportunities for consultants to design behavioral interventions from a variety of behavioral orientations.

A basic premise of behavioral consultation is that behavior is learned; therefore, it can be unlearned and new behavior can take its place. It takes a scientific view of behavior and focuses on current behavior. Change in the client system results from analyzing the client system's behavior in terms of contingencies and developing and implementing a treatment plan to modify behavior (Gallessich, 1983).

Mental Health Consultation

Mental health consultation has its roots in the Freudian framework (Dougherty, 2009b). Gerald Caplan, considered the primary founder of mental health consultation, was a trained psychiatrist. Psychiatrists at the time were heavily influenced by Freud's model. Caplan developed consultation as a preventive method based on his work in preventive psychiatry (Trickett, 1993). Caplan was one of the originators of the terms *primary prevention, secondary prevention,* and *tertiary prevention.* Caplan's intrapsychic views suggested that the work-related problems consultees had with their clients could stem from intrapsychic issues within the consultees themselves as well as within their clients. In his later writings (e.g., Caplan, Caplan, & Erchul, 1994, 2005), he emphasized going beyond the psychodynamic concepts and including organizational and community contexts when providing consultation.

As we will see throughout this volume, Caplan (1970) was one of the first to promote the concept of prevention as it relates to consultation. Caplan was heavily influenced not only by Freud but also by the public health movement of his time. From a mental health perspective, the public health movement focused a great deal on the prevention of mental disorders and the psychological well-being of the community. As noted, terms like *primary prevention* were popularized by Caplan and his colleagues. The popularization of these concepts has had a strong impact on the mental health professions in terms of the perceived need for consultation and how prevention programs are conceptualized and implemented. Mental health consultation was seen as one service among many to prevent or lower the incidence of mental disorders in the community and promote community mental health. The idea is that through consultation the professional competency of the consultee would be enhanced, and fewer referrals would be necessary (Meyers, Brent, Faherty, & Modafferi, 1993).

There are four types of consultation in Caplan's model based on the level at which change is aimed (a case or the organization's administrators) and the primary target of the change effort (client or consultee): (1) Client-centered case consultation is the most frequently used type of mental health consultation. In this type of consultation, the consultant serves as an expert and makes recommendations to the consultee about the case (client). For example, a counseling psychologist observes a student at school and makes written recommendations to a school counselor who is working with the student. (2) Consultee-centered consultation, which has received great attention in the literature, has this major goal: the eliciting of change in consultees so that they are better able to deal not only with the case at hand but also with other similar cases in the future. In one example, a mental health consultant works with another therapist and relies on the therapist's self-reporting to reconceptualize how the consultee chooses to deal with a given client. The consultee is then better able to deal with current and future clients with similar issues. (3) Program-centered administrative consultation is designed to improve glitches in a program or to take on an expert role related to the program such as evaluation. A school counselor, for example, recommends to a principal a method for evaluating a social–emotional learning program at the school. Finally, (4) in consultee-centered administrative consultation, a consultant or consultants work with selected administrators in an organization to resolve problems such as those related to policy and personnel management. The main goal is to bolster the administrators' level of professional functioning so that they can better guide the organization in the future. For example, a mental health consultant facilitates a group of top management of a corporation in developing a team-oriented work climate in the organization. The capacity of the management group is enhanced so that they can deal with similar issues in the future.

Organizational Consultation

Organizational consultation tends to assist organizations to become more effective in terms of the organization's structure and/or process (Dougherty, 2009b). In organizational consultation, the consultant attempts to assist a complex social system (the organization) to be more effective in some way (Illback & Pennington, 2008). For example, a consultant, using the collaborative role, consults with an organization's human resources (HR) department to enhance the quality of its stress prevention program. This type of consultation can occur in any organizational setting.

There is no set theory of organizational consultation. Organizational consultation can focus on one individual within the organization, a group or subset of the organization, or the entire organization (systemwide). The Organization Development (OD) movement has had a strong influence on organizational consultation (Schein, 1988, 2004). A basic promise of OD is to utilize the principles of behavioral science in assisting organizations to be more efficient, more effective, and more resilient. Systems theory is a key element in most organizational consultation (Dougherty, 2009b). Among other premises, system theory assumes that organizations are composed of interacting subsystems, influenced by internal and external forces, and should be considered as a totality when considering change.

Edgar Schein (1988, 2004) popularized three models of organizational consultation: (1) purchase of expertise, (2) doctor–patient, and (3) process. In the purchase of expertise model, the organization has an idea of what is wrong and how to fix it. Therefore, a consultant is called in, or one is used from within the organization to "fix" the problem. For example, in a situation where there is poor morale in an organization, the consultant comes in and works with the organization to raise morale.

In the doctor–patient model, the organization knows something is wrong but is not sure about the nature of the problem. Consultants in this situation assist the organization to determine what is wrong and make recommendations for fixing the problem. Using our example of poor morale from above, the consultant comes in, diagnoses the problem as one of morale, and makes a recommendation for raising morale.

In the process model, the organization knows that something is wrong but is not sure of what the problem is specifically, has constructive intent with regard to solving the problem, and has the capacity to solve the problem once it is diagnosed and an intervention selected. The job of the consultant is to partner with select members of the organization in a collaborative manner to define and solve the problem. In the case of the organization with poor morale, the consultant partners with the members of the organization to determine what the problem is (poor morale) and how to solve that problem. Because the consultee(s) are actively involved throughout the consultation process, this model can have strong preventive effects in that the consultee(s) can learn how to better deal with similar issues in the future with their enhanced problem-solving skills.

Learning Exercise 2

"The Fastest Three Minutes in Consultation"

Pretend you are a television announcer, whose task is to explain to the viewers the similarities and differences among behavioral, mental health, and organizational consultation.

Where would you begin when explaining the similarities and the differences?

3

Research on Consultation

Erchul and Sheridan (2008) noted that the state of scientific research in school consultation is "promising but underdeveloped at present" (p. 3). The same is true for all types of consultation in all settings. There is clearly a large gap between research in consultation and its practice. Irrespective of the limited quality research on consultation, it is effective in terms of outcomes much of the time (Erchul & Sheridan, 2008). The bottom line, however, is that consultation practice has far outpaced the research base of consultation itself.

Consultation research is less than 50 years old, and its sophistication is increasing (Dougherty, 2009b). Reviews of literature regarding consultation (Armenakis & Burdg, 1988; Meade, Hamilton, & Yuen, 1982; Sheridan, Welch, & Orme, 1996) have indicated that it is at least moderately effective.

With all of its research limitations, there has been increased interest in research in consultation, and the quality of current research has improved over the years (Erchul & Sheridan, 2008). Areas such as measurement in consultation research (Schulte, 2008), use of qualitative and mixed methods in research (Meyers, Truscott, Meyers, Varjas, & Collins, 2008), multicultural aspects (Ingraham, 2008), interpersonal influence (Erchul, Grissom, & Getty, 2008), evidence-based research (Frank & Kratochwill, 2008; Kratochwill, 2007), and process and treatment integrity research (Noell, 2008) are receiving increased attention as foci or elements of consultation research.

We previously discussed three models of consultation: (1) behavioral, (2) mental health, and (3) organizational. As you might ascertain, research on these models of consultation is also very limited. Below I provide a brief synopsis of the research on these three models.

Behavioral consultation is the most researched model of consultation (Sheridan et al., 1996). Most of the research conducted on behavioral consultation has been in school settings. Research has demonstrated that behavioral consultation is an effective service in the schools (Martens & DiGennaro, 2008). However, there is little evidence that behavioral consultation is effective in terms of being a preventive approach (Hughes, Loyd, & Buss, 2008).

Compared with behavioral consultation research, mental health consultation has very limited empirical support (Lopez & Nastasi, 2008). One review

(Sheridan et al., 1996) found that only 11% of consultation studies were categorized as mental health consultation, although positive outcomes were reported in 60% of those studies. Furthermore, research in mental health consultation has been criticized for not adequately dealing with efficacy and effectiveness (Knotek, Kaniuka, & Ellingsen, 2008).

Organizational consultation has a very limited research base and, consequently, limited empirical support (Lopez & Nastasi, 2008). The advent of qualitative research and more sophisticated program evaluation measures make the future for developing an evidence base for organizational consultation promising (Illback & Pennington, 2008). One area of organizational consultation that is developing a body of research is in school consultation in the area of positive behavior support (PBS) initiatives (Illback & Pennington, 2008). Little has been written in the organizational consultation literature regarding the preventive aspects of consultation.

In summary, research in consultation, with the exception of behavioral consultation, is limited. Yet with an increasing emphasis on increasing the quality of research in consultation, the future is hopeful.

To what degree has prevention as an aspect of consultation been scrutinized? Unfortunately, the answer is that preventive effects of consultation have not been thoroughly examined (Love, 2007; Zins, 1995). The empirical base for the preventive aspects of consultation is almost nonexistent. The link between consultation and prevention has not received much attention in the consultation literature (Meyers, Meyers, & Grogg, 2004). Correspondingly, empirical research concerning this linkage is limited. For example, research is needed to determine what types of system-level changes are needed to promote preventive consultation (Stoiber & Vanderwood, 2008). In another example, what are the generalizable effects of consultation and how can they be fostered (Meyers et al., 1993)?

Empirically demonstrating the efficacy of consultation, let alone its preventive effects, can be a difficult challenge (Erchul & Martens, 1997). In fact, most of the empirical research conducted on consultation, including prevention in consultation, has been conducted in schools (Erchul & Sheridan, 2008; Zins, 1995).

Much of the research on consultation does not make explicit whether prevention was a goal or examine results from a preventive perspective, thus leading to an ambiguous situation (Zins, 1995). In his review of the literature on the preventive effects of consultation, Zins (1995) explored whether consultation had preventive effects related to the consultee's participation in consultation and also whether consultation is efficacious for delivering prevention programs. Zins concluded the following:

- There is limited but supportive research that suggests that systemwide consultation can be effective in things like decreasing referrals for psychoeducational assessment.

- The preventive effect in terms of modifying consultee attitudes and behavior is of uncertain significance.
- Changes in the clients who were the focus of consultation is not based on solid evidence.
- "There is limited evidence that consultation is an effective practice for delivering preventatively-oriented mental health services." (p. 295)
- In spite of limited empirical evidence, there is strong indication that consultation can be important in delivering prevention programs.
- Empirical evidence supporting the preventive effects of consultation is quite limited but is emerging.

An accurate though brief summary of the research on the preventive aspects of consultation is that "consultation outcome research continues to be largely silent regarding the effectiveness of consultation in preventing problems" (Hughes et al., 2008, p. 348), and "much more research is needed before consultation can be considered a highly valid means of preventing problems" (Love, 2007, p. 168). However, the future for research in this area, like that in consultation in general, is promising. For example, Frank and Kratochwill (2008) argue that research on multitier (i.e., universal, selected, and indicated levels) models will better assess the preventive effects of consultation.

4

Consultation and Prevention

onsultation can be a strong force in advancing prevention (Strein & Koehler, 2008), and it has strong roots in prevention (Zins, 1995). Consultation, being an indirect service, can assist in the prevention of psychological problems and can be used to promote the psychological well-being of others. Consultation "is widely assumed to aid in the prevention of problems and in the promotion of mental health" (Zins, 1995, p. 285). It is assumed that the beneficial effects of consultation on the consultee generalize to assist the consultee to be more effective with similar situations in the future and in the prevention of problems (Dougherty, 2009b). Hence, the consultation experience allows the consultee to have a transfer of effect or a generalization of lessons learned (behaviorally and/or attitudinally; Alpert, 1976) to new, similar situations. As a result of this preventive effect, the consultee becomes an agent of prevention from having gone through consultation. This suggests that the preventive impact of consultation can be maximized when consultees are significantly engaged in all aspects of the consultation process.

Consultation's remedial capacity is most often emphasized while ignoring its potential to bolster consultee capacity building, and these roots have often been ignored in the literature and practice (Kelly, 1993; Meyers et al., 2004). For example, the literature on organizational consultation has not emphasized prevention (Caplan et al., 1994). Most of the literature about consultation and prevention stems from Albee's (1980, 1982, 1985) proposition that mental health services should focus on primary prevention of problems' occurrence rather than exclusively on their remediation and Caplan's (1961, 1964, 1970, 1974) ideas regarding public health–oriented preventive mental health services.

The linkage between consultation and prevention, however, was articulated in the community mental health movement (Caplan, 1993; Snow & Swift, 1985). Prevention of mental illness, for example, was a federal initiative in community mental health, and consultation was a mandated service. Mental health consultation was developed to assist professionals to integrate mental health principles into their work (Caplan, 1993). Consultation itself can have preventive effects, and as importantly, prevention programs frequently rely on consultation as a service to enhance their effectiveness (Zins, 1995).

Caplan's influence on prevention and its subsequent impact of consultation is significant. Consultation, it is important to note, was only one element among many in a paradigm of prevention popularized by Caplan. He viewed consultation as one important service along with others such as preventive psychiatry, population-oriented prevention, support systems, and primary prevention programming, all of which would reduce mental health issues and promote mental health in the community (Caplan, Caplan, & Erchul, 1994). As Caplan viewed it, all of these elements were designed to be "health promoting forces at the person-to-person and social levels which enable people to master the challenges and strains of their lives" (Caplan, 1974, p. vii). Caplan, therefore, saw prevention from both the individual person and social institution perspectives. Prevention attempts, then, could be targeted at individual as well as the ecological milieu in which individuals interacted.

Caplan (1974) used the term *support system* to describe one of many social groups that could assist with primary prevention. The idea is that social support could act as a buffer protecting the individual from environmental stressors that precipitate mental illness, and it could also be a force to promote mental health. Consultants, when promoting prevention, could capitalize on the use of support systems in organizations and with individuals in maximizing the effects of prevention. The effects of consultation, for example, could lead to the creation of employee assistance programs (EAP) in an organization. In consulting at the individual level, an example is a mental health professional consulting with a family therapist on better ways to strengthen the consultee's client (a family) so that the members support each other consistently and communicate effectively with one another. As can be seen, mental health consultation itself is a support system.

Caplan noted that while mental health consultants are often cast into the expert role in creating or maintaining support system, he also felt that other members of the community (e.g., clergymen) could take on this expert role when properly trained. Caplan also felt that many so-called nonprofessional caregivers could also benefit from consultee-centered consultation (see below) and achieve competence without direct education/training due to their high levels of experience. Caplan went on to point out that community caregivers would encounter the unexpected when trying to be part of a support system. In this case, he recommended mental health consultation.

It should be noted at the outset that a great deal of the literature on prevention and consultation has been developed around school-based consultation, even though other disciplines have contributed to the development of consultation (Zins, 1995). This is due in part to the fact that there has been an increasing emphasis in professions such as school counseling and school psychology toward systems-level thinking and change and proactivity (Sheridan & Gutkin, 2000; Tilly, 2008) that lend themselves well to prevention activities. Increasingly, school-based mental health professionals as well as external consultants who work with schools have adopted prevention as one major role in providing services, including consultation (Strein & Koehler, 2008). This body of literature sheds a great deal of light on consultation and prevention in nonschool settings.

Consultation can serve as a tool for the implementation of primary, secondary, and tertiary prevention (Parsons & Meyers, 1984). The majority of our discussion will discuss consultation as one process to implement primary and secondary prevention. Although in the past, there has been reluctance on the part of organizations to invest in prevention practices such as consultation (Parsons & Meyers, 1984) due to the emphasis on remediation and the difficulty in assessing prevention efforts, there has been a significant increase in preventive consultation in the past 3 decades. Three general areas of primary prevention for which consultation can be used include analysis and modification of social environments, development of competence and adaptive practices, and stress reduction (Parsons & Meyers, 1984).

It is important to try to prevent behavioral and emotional issues in any population. Preventive application can yield a reduction in the occurrence of new cases of a problem and in the duration and severity of incipient problems, and it can promote strengths, optimal healthy human functioning, and healthy environments (Conyne, 2004). In addition, when preventive consultation is effective, the need for resources and services diminishes (Love, 2007). The sources of the positive effects of consultation are typically due to the importation of new expertise, capacity, persistence, and care into a system (Erchul & Sheridan, 2008).

Prevention can include universal applications such as an entire organization or elements within a certain population that are at risk, like children of divorce. Preventive interventions are often delivered as part of a larger "package" (e.g., multitiered) of services that include remedial and crisis-related interventions. One of the reasons for this is that "a multi-tiered service delivery model emphasizes the prevention of problems by creating environments of prevention" (Hojnoski, 2007, p. 158) less in need of reactive, individual-level interventions. For example, a school that blends academic instruction with a prevention program designed to have students develop interpersonal communication skills may well affect its social climate in such a way that incidences of aggressive behavior among students decline significantly and academic achievement increases correspondingly.

The goals of universal interventions include strengthening protective factors (e.g., positive communication system in an organization), preventing problems before their occurrence (e.g., building morale among employees), and offering a wide range of resources to members of the social system who are at risk (e.g., an EAP; Christner, Mennuti, & Whitaker, 2009). Consultation can play an important role in helping organizations to meet these goals when they implement universal interventions. In addition, consultants can provide expertise in assessing preventive goals in a variety of ways, including training staff to conduct focus groups, developing and conducting surveys, reviewing organizational data relative to the preventive goals, and providing technical reports based on all of the assessment data gathered.

As we will see, one basic way to implement preventive consultation is to engage in consultee-centered case consultation (Parsons & Meyers, 1984) and, thereby, build consultees' skills (Zins, 1995). By focusing on the positive growth of consultees, consultee-centered case consultation develops the knowledge bases and skill sets of consultees to more effectively equip them to deal with similar cases in the future.

We will also discuss another way to implement preventive consultation: through systemwide consultation. Systemwide consultation has the potential to have the greatest preventive effect of all types of consultation due to its broad and pervasive impact (Parsons, 1996; Parsons & Meyers, 1984; Zins, 1995). Consultation using a systemwide approach can enhance the preventive capacity of a system by enhancing all or one of the following: the elements of the system, such as the people in it; the structure and operational characteristics of the system, such as patterns of communications; and the forces affecting the system, such as its community advisory board (Parsons & Meyers, 1984). By changing the goals, frameworks, and/or operations of the system, more lasting change and concomitant preventative impact is possible (Parsons, 1996).

In conclusion, the increase in the incidences of emotional/behavioral problems and issues in our society, along with the decreasing numbers of mental health professionals to address these issues, demands that the field of consultation more effectively develop its preventive elements. The effectiveness of agencies, or any organization for that matter, can be enhanced through preventive consultation. For example, our schools see more and more students with emotional, behavioral, and family issues that impede their academic learning (Christner et al., 2009). While we certainly need to deal with the mental health problems as they arise in our schools' students, we must as importantly use preventive measures such as teaching students coping skills to meet life's issues (Christner et al., 2009).

Preventive Consultation in Action: An Example of Enhancing Mental Health Services in Schools

An illustration of consultation's preventive benefits is an example of reducing the marginalization of mental health programs in schools. Reducing the marginalization of mental health services in schools entails reworking policy, reframing intervention under a unifying concept, rethinking the organizational and operational infrastructure at all levels of the school system, and facilitating systemic change in schools (Adelman & Taylor, 2009).

At the policy level, consultants can provide assistance to local policy makers in reworking policy to reflect mental health initiatives as ways to promote effective teaching and learning. At a more pragmatic level, consultants can take on a collaborative role with selected school personnel in analyzing current school policies and making recommendations related to coordination of services for neutralizing issues (e.g., poor attendance) that negatively affect teaching and learning.

In reframing interventions, consultants can assist schools in refocusing priorities from focusing on services for students in need to improving schools for all students. In other words, the school, rather than a few selected students, constitutes the client system (Adelman & Taylor, 2009). In one example, Adelman and Taylor (2009) point out the importance of having interventions for promoting healthy development and preventing problems and systems for early intervention for at-risk populations.

Rethinking the infrastructure of a school or school district provides a great many opportunities for preventive consultation. Such change will eliminate social forces that lead to social–emotional problems in students. Changes in infrastructure are the logical mechanisms that will be put into place to implement the aforementioned changes in policy (Adelman & Taylor, 2009). For example, a school district, under the facilitation of a consultant, could determine to convert its junior high schools to middle schools in order to provide a more student-centered climate.

In enabling systemic change, consultants with a preventive orientation can take on the collaborative role and assist personnel in schools (and any other type of organization) in dealing with the four overlapping elements of systemic change (Adelman & Taylor, 2009): (1) creating readiness, (2) initial implementation, (3) institutionalization and ongoing evaluation, and (4) creative renewal. Preventive methods include training of decision makers in planning for change, coaching on progress of change initiatives, and evaluation of change efforts.

In a nonschool example, Schmidt, Hoffman, and Taylor (2006) discussed the potential of consultation with professionals working with patients and clients with HIV/AIDS. Consultants could point out the implications of related research findings. The authors note that "such consultation would keep the community agency on the cutting edge of information about HIV/AIDS and the most effective interventions, ultimately enhancing their ability to provide quality services to the community" (p. 365). In another example, Hojnoski (2007) points out the possibility that in school environments PBS (Sugai & Horner, 2008) and social and emotional learning programs (SEL; Zins & Elias, 2006) both have the potential for preventing problems when used with consultation.

PBS is an approach to intervention based on positive psychology. It uses interventions at the individual, classroom, or schoolwide level or some combination of these three levels to promote positive and socially important behavior change using empirically validated procedures (Sugai et al., 2000). SEL is "the capacity to recognize and manage emotions, solve problems effectively, and establish positive relationships with others, competencies that clearly are essential for all students" (Zins & Elias, 2006, p. 234). There are many programs that teach students the skill sets involved in SEL.

As noted above, PBS is not only a good example of reducing the *marginalization* of mental health programs in the schools but also an excellent example of *developing* exemplary mental health. School-based consultants can be integrally involved in organizational activities for implementing mental health programs like PBS (Nastasi & Varjas, 2008). Nastasi and Varjas (2008), for example, introduced a model, the Participatory Culture-Specific Intervention Model, for effective implementation of system-level programs. School-based consultants can be involved in program implementation in a variety of ways, ranging from facilitating the formation of partnerships to modeling and/or conducting program evaluation and from assisting stakeholders to determine the nature of the types of data needed relative to defining the culture of the school to participating in formative research to ensure that the program is on track in meeting its goals.

Consultation with population-based school mental health services can amplify those programs' preventive effects. Examples include consulting with teachers regarding behavioral adjustments of students; collaborating with school administrators and pertinent staff in ensuring safe school environments such as lunchrooms, bathrooms, and playground areas; and assisting administrators and school teams in refining school discipline policies and procedures (Doll & Cummings, 2008). Such activities add to prevention because they promote conditions in which there will be a staff knowledgeable about and skilled in dealing with student issues, an environment that is safe and perceived as safe by all members of the school, and a consistent set of procedures and policies that school members know about, understand, and adhere to.

Learning Exercise 3

"Take Two"

You have just read about the connection between consultation and prevention. Please reread that section again and then play "Take Two."

Directions for "Take Two": Think about what you have just read about consultation and prevention. Now pretend that you have been asked by a well-known social networking website to post the two most important connections between consultation and prevention under a posting named "Take Two."

Below, list the two most important connections in your opinion and provide a two sentence rationale for each of your choices.

Consultation/Prevention Connection 1

_____

_____

_____

_____

_____

Rationale: _____

_____

_____

_____

_____

Consultation/Prevention Connection 2

_____

_____

_____

_____

_____

Rationale: _____

_____

_____

_____

_____

_____ Consultation Models Emphasizing Prevention

While all models of consultation have a preventive aspect, some models stand out in their potential to have powerful preventive effects. I discuss these below.

Consultee-Centered Consultation

A classic consultation model that can emphasize prevention is consultee-centered consultation, a type of mental health consultation (Caplan, 1970; Caplan & Caplan, 1993). Consultee-centered consultation can take the form of case and administrative consultation. A detailed discussion of consultee-centered consultation is beyond the scope of this volume (readers are referred to Dougherty, 2009b, for a detailed explanation). These are the most indirect types of mental health consultation and, as a result, have the most potential for preventive impact (Kelly, 1993). Caplan originally developed mental health consultation as a primary prevention intervention, and both types of consultee-centered consultation allow consultants to work with organizations and individual caregivers to lower the incidence of mental disorders in the population (Caplan & Caplan-Moskovich, 2004).

In consultee-centered case consultation, when consultants assist consultees "to find a solution to their current work impasse, the experience will have a long term carryover to improving their professional effectiveness" (Caplan & Caplan-Moskovich, 2004, p. 34). By understanding their clients from different perspectives, consultees are actually engaging in a professional development experience that will assist them in the future (Babinski, Knotek, & Rogers, 2004; Sandoval, 2004a, 2004b). In consultee-centered consultation, consultants can support a preventive effect by enhancing one or more of the consultee's competencies: knowledge, skills, confidence, and objectivity (Gongora, 2004).

As a prevention service, the consultant helps the consultee with a case of concern to the consultee. As a result of consultation, the consultee is empowered to generalize the learning from consultation to similar cases in the future (Lambert, 2004). The consultee-centered consultation process results in a broader, more comprehensive view of the client, which results in a more effective professional functioning on the part of the consultee. The main goal of consultee-centered consultation is to remediate the professional shortcomings of the consultee. The secondary goal is to help the client.

Many times, consultees must first "demonstrate readiness to engage in consultation and be reinforced for doing so" (Blom-Huffman & Rose, 2007, p. 152). One method of increasing the probability of active engagement by consultees, and thus maximizing the preventive effects of consultation, is the use of motivational interviewing (Miller & Rollnick, 2002). Motivational interviewing "is an evidence-based consultation style that increases peoples' readiness to change by helping them resolve ambivalence" (Blom-Huffman & Rose, 2007, p. 152). This method can assist consultees to positively view the fact that in order to change a client system's behavior, they too must change theirs. Basically, motivational interviewing recognizes that it is difficult for humans to change their behavior. People tend to be ambivalent about changing their behavior because they are getting some type of reward for engaging in undesirable behavior even though they know that they need to change. By being empathic and helping consultees explore their cases or programs from a variety of perspectives, motivational interviewing can increase the level of commitment for change on the part of the consultee.

Cognitive modeling is another approach that may enhance the preventive effects of consultation (Gutkin, 1993). Cognitive modeling may help improve the problem-solving skills of the consultee, thus promoting prevention. The idea is that the consultant makes the covert problem-solving processes explicit for the consultee, thus increasing the chances that the consultee will imitate the consultant's behavior and thereby become a more effective problem solver on his or her own. This modeling process can be incorporated into the consultation process without difficulty. An example of consultee-centered case consultation involves a mental health professional consulting with another therapist about the therapist's subjective view of the case. The consultant assists the consultee to reframe his or her thinking about the case, thus assisting the therapist to work more effectively with the case. The therapist might have been thinking that the only way to be successful with the case was to have the client deal with the anger issues being discussed in the therapy sessions. By focusing on the case and looking at alternative methodologies, the therapist's thinking is expanded and new ways of conceptualizing and intervening in the case are discovered. The focal issue is no longer the client's anger, but new ways of effectively resolving the client's issues, such as developing conflict management skills, are dealt with. In an example, a consultant makes explicit to the consultee the stages and phases of the consulting process (Dougherty, 2009b). In diagnosing the problem, the consultant explains to the client that this outcome will consist of gathering information, defining the problem, setting related goals, and generating possible interventions. As they go through the various phases, the consultant again makes explicit what they have just done, the results of those actions, and what the consultant and consultee are going to do next in the consultation. The consultee, as a result of cognitive modeling by the consultant, is better able to problem solve in the future.

Finally, in consultee-centered administrative consultation, a consultant or consultants work with selected administrators in an organization to resolve organizational problems, such as those related to policy and personnel management. Consultee-centered consultation can move beyond assisting the individual caregiver and assist a caregiving institution to improve its policies and procedures so that its clients are better served and, hence, promoting prevention (Caplan & Caplan-Moskovich, 2004). The main goal is to bolster the administrators' level of professional functioning so that they guide the organization better in the future. In consultee-centered administrative consultation, the mental health professional works with an organization's administrative personnel to increase the level of their professional functioning. The focus of the consultation is a particular issue within the organization, such as difficulty in implementing a prevention program, but the primary goal is to increase the administrators' skill sets in dealing with the aforementioned program and similar programs in the future. In an example, a mental health consultant works with the administrators of a community-sponsored program for abused women. The consultant "roams" through the organization and assists in defining issues and gathering data. In addition, the consultant uses the collaborative role in creating with the administrators additional programs that deal with crises that may emerge while the program is being implemented. This approach not only improved administrator functioning with the given issue but also had the preventive effect of providing the administrators with competence in dealing with crisis issues that could emerge now and in the future with other programs.

Models Emphasizing Positive Psychology

Some authors (Akin-Little, Little, & Delligatti, 2004; Meyers et al., 2004; Meyers & Nastasi, 1999) have developed school-based models of consultation that emphasize prevention using positive psychology (e.g., Compton, 2005; Seligman & Csikszentmihalyi, 2000). These models suggest that positive psychology is a useful concept in enhancing the preventive effects of consultation. Rather than focusing on deficits and liabilities of individuals, positive psychology focuses on their strengths. This focus on the positive has important implications for consultation as it can lead to increased attention toward developing social skills, resilience, and enhanced self-esteem.

The preventative consultation model developed by Akin-Little et al. (2004) utilizes the principles of positive psychology, which are synthesized with behavioral consultation and mental health consultation. In this model, the consultant assists consultees in the development and implementation of their personal positive psychology (using mental health consultation and focusing on consultee strengths) and then works with consultees to implement positive psychology principles in working with their client system(s) (using behavioral consultation). The subsequent use of positive reinforcement (due to changes in attitudes and behavior) by consultees is assumed to prevent problems from occurring in their client systems.

The model of preventive consultation developed by Meyers and Nastasi (1999) utilizes both positive psychology and public health concepts, including ecological principles. These authors have modified Caplan's concepts of primary, secondary, and tertiary prevention to entail primary prevention, risk reduction, early intervention, and treatment. In these authors' model, primary prevention refers to preventing problems in an entire population. Risk reduction deals with preventing problems in at-risk populations. Early intervention attempts to eradicate problems that are emergent. Treatment has the purpose of alleviating existing problems and minimizing their impact on others.

This preventive consultation model is distinguished among client-centered, consultee-centered, and system-centered consultation and utilizes group as well as individual approaches. The system-centered model (see below) is the most indirect and has the potential to have the broadest preventive impact. Group consultation can be of two types. One type is when there is one consultant and a group of consultees. This allows the consultant to maximize preventive effects through working with multiple individuals simultaneously. A second type of preventive consultation occurs when a group of consultants work with an individual consultee. Prereferral intervention teams in schools are an example of this type of group consultation.

Organizational Models

Prevention can be promoted in consulting with organizations in a variety of ways (Meyers et al., 2004). Organizational consultation promotes prevention by focusing on a system such as an entire school, thus creating the opportunity for risk reduction (e.g., programs for children of divorce) or primary prevention (e.g., social skills training). Organizational consultation is particularly amenable to public health principles that focus on implementing primary prevention and risk reduction interventions aimed at an entire system. That said, organizational consultation can be effective in working at different levels within an organization. For example, in consultee-centered consultation, prevention can be enhanced by working with consultees to change their behavior in which they focus on changing selected environments (e.g., a classroom) rather than an individual client (Knotek et al., 2008).

Mental health consultation that emphasizes prevention within organizations has been proposed by Caplan (1970) and then adapted by Caplan et al. (1994). These authors view preventive consultation as underutilized in organizations; however, the potential for preventive consultation to positively affect organization is tremendous. These authors note, "We see the organizational setting as an excellent one in which to carry out an agenda of primary prevention" (Caplan et al., 1994, p. 6). Mental health consultation in organizations can be used to affect lasting positive changes. Consultants can promote prevention in addition to taking a remedial view when dealing with the issues brought for consultation. The typical issues that organizations experience, such as employee absenteeism, are often termed *crises* in the primary prevention literature and offer opportunities for consultants to promote prevention. There are three methods for promoting prevention on the part of consultants. The first method is to reduce the intensity and duration of stressors within the organization that defeat attainment of organizational goals. Second, consultants can assist organizations to develop an anticipatory set about possible issues and crises, and then develop a plan for dealing with their occurrence. For example, improving strategic planning in an organization can lead to anticipating the prevention programs needed (Knoff & Batsche, 1993). Third, consultants can work to "mobilize psychosocial supports" (Caplan et al., 1994, p. 9) for use when members of the organization are in stressful situations. Table 4.1 illustrates these methods and provides a related example.

Table 4.1   Relationship Between Mental Health Consultation With Organizations and Prevention

Prevention Goal	Consultation Example	Primary Prevention Effect
Reduce the intensity and duration of counterproductive organizational stressors	Consultant collaborates with management to improve the communication system to assist all employees to know what is expected of them and how their work ties into the organization's goals.	Organization's infrastructure supports positive work climate and employees' psychological growth.
Develop capacity to respond effectively to expected and unexpected crises	Consultant, using a collaborative role, assists an organization's HR Department to develop, disseminate, and integrate a crisis intervention plan within organization.	Crises are as anticipated as possible and managed with a plan that includes the well being of the organization's members.
Mobilize psychosocial supports within the organization	Consultant collaborates with the leadership of an organization to develop and integrate an EAP designed to promote mental health among employees.	Active emotion and work-related support systems are available and unitized by the organization.

Application: The Scope of Consultation and Prevention Programs_____

Consultation can contribute to prevention programs (Zins, 1995). For example, consultants can assist prevention programs by taking on a variety of roles, such as the collaborative role in assisting in the actual program implementation, in working with the program's support system, and in analyzing the context of the intervention (see Greenberg, Domitrovich, Gracyzk, & Zins, 2001; Tanyu, 2007). Consultation can be used to ensure that elements considered essential for prevention programs such as those cited by Zins and Elias (2006) are dealt with: developing a systems-level view of the environment in which the program takes place, assisting with the human dynamics related to program implementation, enhancing the skills of the people involved, and assisting with policy making that supports the program. In other words, the impact of consultation on prevention programs can be strongest when it involves system-level concepts, empowers the people involved, and builds on their strengths.

Consultation can also be used to ensure quality control in the delivery of prevention services (Caplan & Caplan, 1994). Strein and Koelher (2008), in referring to internal consultants, point out that involvement in prevention programs will go more smoothly if the consultants already have a history of involvement in case-centered or team-centered consultation and provide ongoing consultative support during prevention programs. In addition, program participants, when involved in the design, implementation, and evaluation of the program, can add to the preventive effects of consultation because of their involvement as well as enhanced skill development from being involved in these activities. Below, I cite several examples of consultation contributing to the efficacy of prevention programs.

Community Outreach

Consultation was part of a community outreach prevention program that was developed in response to the needs of an urban, predominantly Latino population in a large midwestern city (Vera, Daly, Gonzales, Morgan, & Thakral, 2006). The program had three components: (1) classroom-based prevention programming for students (psychoeducational with exploration of adolescent issues and strengthening personal and academic competencies), (2) workshops for parents (culturally sensitive parenting practices), (3) and consultations with the teachers and administrators. The consultation sessions were held before school and lasted approximately 45 minutes. Vera et al. (2006) report that

> the teachers' consultations involved 45-minute sessions before school. During these sessions, facilitators would help teachers identify mental health needs of their students and help them understand the cultural

context factors involved in the development of academic and personal problems. Often, the session content was case example-based, where teachers discussed specific students, or types of students, about whom they were all concerned. (p. 92)

Social Justice

Consultation has been involved in the promotion of social justice by consulting directly with school personnel (Davidson, Waldo, & Adams, 2006). Two prevention projects made up the program. The Safe School Project provided sensitivity training regarding lesbians, gays, bisexuals, and transgender people to school psychologists, counselors, nurses, and social workers and provided expertise in developing "safe zones." The Supporting Teachers Supporting Students program helped teachers to develop the skills and knowledge to help students overcome barriers to their learning. Consultants used the train-the-trainer approach, whereby participants learned to conduct workshops that promoted problem prevention and social justice for rural, poor minority youth.

Li and Vazquez-Nuttall (2009) describe how school-based consultants can act as agents of social justice for multicultural children and families. The authors make suggestions for interventions at the individual, classroom, home–school relationships, professional, and social policy–setting levels. Prevention can be promoted at any of these levels, particularly those that are more encompassing such as the social policy setting.

Shaping Public Policy

Consultation can be useful in shaping social policy and popular thinking (Bell & Goodman, 2006). The Victim-Informed Prosecution Project focused on both offender accountability and victim safety. Consultation was provided on both individual cases, and additional consultation dealt with how the emotional and physical safety needs of battered women might affect their involvement with the court system. These authors concluded that basic consultation skills are necessary for effectively influencing social policy and popular thinking. They note, for example, that in developing an official report and recommendations for the city on the evaluation of their project, they took into account "how to acknowledge both the strengths and weaknesses of the current system, how to present our participants' ideas in a way that would be heard, and what might be the most feasible way to implement the study's results" (p. 166). The consultants also provided their expertise to the parties involved on how they might form more trusting relationships with the victims with whom they were dealing with. In one final consultative activity, the authors "shared with the team measures and protocols that they could use to more accurately assess each participant's mental health and history of abuse" (p. 166).

International Settings

Preventive consultation in international settings, particularly as it relates to social justice, has also received attention (Horne & Mathews, 2006). Note the strong emphasis on the collaborative focus of the consultants. Emphasis on consultee input and expertise is essential as "consultees generally want consultants to know 'enough' so that it is evident that they have some contextual understanding, but consultees also wish to retain their expert positions on their experience" (p. 391). These authors point out that to facilitate positive interaction between consultants and consultees, an understanding of global power is paramount. The authors go on to present a multicultural-feminist consultation model that focuses on collaborative as opposed to expert consultation. That said, this model presents content throughout the process, with the consultant resonating back and forth between content and process. Consultants need to be alert to cultural differences that are indicated by issues such as language barriers. Consultants in this model emphasize prevention through the use of advocacy for implementing a social justice agenda when possible as well as help consultees explore important issues within and without the organization that impede organizational goals and use networking to maintain consultees' linkages to other social agendas in other organizations.

Peer Consultation Program

McWhirter and McWhirter (2006) present a "couples helping couples" program in Chile, which illustrates an international consultation program that uses prevention interventions such as training to implement a social justice agenda. By training and providing close consultation to groups called "Mentor Couples" (p. 407) through the context of a family faith education program, consultants prepare the mentor couples to assist other couples to be educators and role models for faith for their children.

Bullying Prevention

Orpinas and Horne (2006) describe the School Social Competence Development and Bullying Prevention Model. This model emphasizes both the enhancement of school climate and the development of social competence in students. There is extensive opportunity for consultants with a preventive orientation to take on a variety of roles when consulting with school personnel in the development and implementation of this model in individual schools.

Resilience

Brehm and Doll (2009) describe a variety of prevention programs aimed at building resilience in schools. Regardless of the type of prevention program, consultants can provide a variety of services. In one example, a consultant assists a school district in selecting and implementing a school resilience program. In another example, a consultant, using a collaborative role, facilitates selected members of a school district in determining how best to integrate a school resilience-building program into its other universal mental health initiatives.

Positive Behavior Support

Farrell (2009) reports of the use of schoolwide PBS. PBS programs can have universal, targeted, and individual supports. Internal consultants such as school psychologists and school counselors can be effective in preparing school personnel for PBS program implementation. In one example, a school psychologist is tasked with developing personnel teams for implementing the PBS program at each grade level. In another example, an external consultant, a mental health professional, engages in fact-finding to determine the level of competence needed by school personnel to effectively implement the program. Selected school personnel, under the consultant's facilitation, develop plans to bring all parties to the desired competency level.

Social Competence

Developing social competence in students as a way of preventing mental health problems and fostering human development has received increasing attention (Barbarasch & Elias, 2009). Enhanced SEL among a student body, as well as school personnel, can lead to a decrease in problems such as bullying while fostering skills for successful living. SEL can be fostered through a variety of multitiered programs. Consultants, for example, can help schools modify existing SEL programs to ensure a good cultural fit to the school (Barbarasch & Elias, 2009). Also, consultants can aid in SEL program selection by analyzing evidenced-based support for given programs and by determining the financial cost of their implementation.

Learning Exercise 4

"The Choice Is Yours"
    You have been given the opportunity to work with any two of the programs mentioned above in this section. Which of the programs would you choose based on the limited information you have?

First choice program:_____

_____

_____

_____

Rationale:_____

_____

_____

_____

Second choice program:_____

_____

_____

_____

_____

Rationale:_____

_____

_____

_____

_____

5

Illustrative Examples

Illustrative Example 1: Consultation in Bullying and Mobbing Prevention in the Workplace

Bullying and mobbing are common phenomena in all types of workplace settings (Sperry, 2009b). While bullying and mobbing in schools are clearly problems, particularly among students (Felix & Furlong, 2008), they are also a major workplace concern for most organizations (Fox & Stallworth, 2009). Beyond the harm to the victims of bullying and mobbing (e.g., health and psychological maladies), these forms of abusiveness cost organizations large sums of dollars due to events such as medical costs and absenteeism (Ferris, 2009). Consultants can play a significant role in working with organizations to prevent these forms of abusiveness (Sperry, 2009a), thus creating a more respectful workplace.

While bullying and mobbing are on the increase in the workplace, there are still no agreed on definitions of bullying and mobbing. One practice is to view bullying and mobbing on a continuum with bullying being a milder type of abusive behavior relative to mobbing (Sperry, 2009a). Both involve the "persistent and repeated targeting of an individual with the goal of harming them or their work" (Ferris, 2009, p. 172). One more specific definition cites workplace bullying as "behavior that threatens, intimidates, humiliates, or isolates people at work, or undermines their reputation or job performance" (Fox & Stallworth, 2009, p. 220). Ferris (2009) adds that both bullying and mobbing "involve a pattern of repeated hostile verbal and nonverbal interactions that are generally nonphysical and directed at a target, resulting in a negative impact on the target's sense of self as a competent worker or person" (p. 171). Bullying and mobbing usually involve some form of power imbalance, either formal or informal. People who are perpetrators in bullying or mobbing tend to possess traits such as the need to protect self-esteem, lack of social efficacy such as anger management, and "micropolitical behavior" (behavior designed to protect one's own goals within the organization; Zapf & Einarsen, 2003).

By looking at some of the explanations of bullying and mobbing in the workplace, we will get a sense of the scope of interventions in which consultants can engage in preventing their occurrence. In explaining workplace bullying and mobbing, Sperry (2009a, 2009b) makes an analogy utilizing the concepts of "bad apple," "bad apples," and "bad barrel" and their interaction. When looked at from the perspective of preventive consultation, the idea is to prevent having a "bad apple," "bad apples," or a "bad barrel" in the first place.

The "bad apple" perspective views the individual dynamics of the abuser, such as personality or work orientation, as the cause of any workplace abuse such as bullying. That said, there is little empirical evidence regarding the personal characteristics of victims and perpetrators relative to bullying (Sperry, 2009a).

The "bad apples" explanation suggests that a *group* of employees deliberately plan and execute behaviors designed to abuse a fellow worker. This concept assumes that people in the workplace are part of formal and/or informal teams and that both types of teams are instrumental in accomplishing the work of the organization (Sperry, 2009a). Work group dynamics strongly influence whether bullying and/or mobbing will result. For example, when group cohesion is low, the quality of group functioning can suffer. In another example, informal groups can develop an agenda that focuses on disruption of organizational goals that leads to bullying and mobbing of other workers.

The "bad barrel" perspective suggests toxic influences in the organizational dynamics that lead to bullying and/or mobbing. Organizational dynamics include the interaction of forces operating on the subsystems of the organization. Organizational dynamics can be key indicators of the existence or potential for bullying and mobbing (Sperry, 2009a). For example, Sperry (1996, 2009a) notes that one view of organizational subsystems entails structure, culture, strategy, leaders, and the organization's external environment. The dynamics within each of these subsystems have the power to influence the occurrence or prevention of bullying and mobbing. For example, different types of bullying and mobbing occur in the lower levels of the organization as opposed to the middle and higher levels (structural subsystem). In another example, leaders of the organization can be actively or passively complicit on the occurrence of bullying and mobbing or may be advocates for their prevention (leadership subsystem).

By understanding how each of these views and their possible interactions promote workplace abuse, consultants can plan for effective preventive efforts. Sperry (2009a) suggests that individual dynamics, group dynamics, and organizational dynamics (or their interaction) can promote workplace bullying and mobbing and, hence, are the target of preventive (as well as remedial) efforts. By focusing on these sets of dynamics and their interplay, consultants can employ assessment and intervention techniques that promote the prevention of bullying and mobbing.

In another conceptualization, Ferris (2009) adds that it is important for consultants to be knowledgeable concerning the antecedents of bullying and mobbing in order to effectively assist in their prevention. These antecedents are the individual characteristics, social factors facilitating bullying/mobbing, and organizational features.

Individual factors that lead to perpetration include the need to maintain self-esteem, lack of social skill sets such as control of frustration, and "micropolitical behavior" (Ferris, 2009, p. 175), which, as noted above, relates to positioning oneself in the work environment in order to meet one's agenda. Social variables that are antecedents to bullying/mobbing include conditions such as perceived unfairness, frustration at work, and workplace stress. Organizational antecedents include a variety of factors including leadership behavior, organizational climate and culture, and ambiguity and conflict in role implementation. Namie and Namie (2009) corroborate the fact that top leadership is instrumental in preventing bullying/mobbing due to their shaping of the organization's culture through their decision-making processes.

The Role of the Consultant in the Prevention of Workplace Bullying and Mobbing

As we will see below, consultants can play a significant role in preventing the occurrence of workplace bullying and mobbing. Consultants can provide interventions at one or all of the levels of an organization: individual, group, and organization-wide (Namie & Namie, 2009). Possible consultant interventions include "surveillance, policy development, training, coaching, and the development of selection, performance management, and reward systems that set standards for collaborative and supportive behavior at work" (Ferris, 2009, p. 169). Examples at the individual level include consultee-centered case and consultee-centered administrative consultation (Caplan & Caplan, 1993). Consultants can implement systemwide prevention strategies, for example, related to improving the quality of work life in the organization (Ferris, 2009).

Consultation at the Individual Level. Consultants can take on a preventive role by being actively engaged in the resolution of bullying/mobbing events. By engaging in consultee-centered consultation, consultants can assist their consultees in reframing how they are approaching the resolution process and the parties involved so that the chances of any party being involved in a subsequent bullying/mobbing event are diminished. For example, a consultant could assist mediators to see beyond the view that a perpetrator's actions are just "due to the way they are," or help other mediators come to understand that a victim "just doesn't ask for abuse by the way he/she behaves at work." Mediation can be a risky intervention in organizations whose culture inadvertently facilitates bullying/mobbing (Namie & Namie, 2009). However, when appropriate, peer facilitation training of employees in mediation for mild conflicts by consultants is an effective preventive intervention.

Consultants often engage in leadership coaching as a means to prevent workplace bullying/mobbing (Ferris, 2009). Such coaching typically involves leadership training (knowledge, skills, and attitudes) for creating a respectful work environment and effective enforcement methods for dealing with any incidences (potential or otherwise) related to bullying/mobbing. Behavioral checklists assessing bullying potential are often used with leaders themselves as a means of assisting them to see their own potential for bullying and, hence, promoting their personal growth (Ferris, 2009). Support in terms of developing tactics and rehearsing preventive behavior sets based on manager needs is also effective (Namie & Namie, 2009). Namie and Namie (2009) list three forms for executive coaching in workplace bullying/mobbing. One form is assisting managers in using confrontation as an intervention in dealing with perpetrators. This type of coaching can have possible preventive effects if word that reports of workplace abuse will be handled forcefully by the powers-to-be goes through the formal and informal structures of the organization. A second form of coaching involves educating managers about the negative implications of the presence of bullying in their organization. Coaching of this type can have a preventative impact by helping managers to see the importance of a policy on workplace bullying/mobbing and, thus, promote them to develop a policy and/or more effectively emphasize an existing policy. A third type of coaching helps prepare the manager to implement policies and procedures related to bullying/mobbing. A possible preventive effect of this type of coaching is public support and promotion of the policy throughout the organization, which informs the members of the organization that bullying/mobbing do not lead to a productive organization and, therefore, are not tolerated.

Consultation at the Group Level. Clearly, training of groups of key personnel by consultants can be a powerful force in the prevention of bullying/mobbing at the workplace (Ferris, 2009). Training often takes the form of hands-on workshops that educate about bullying/mobbing, provide skills training in preventing and managing their occurrence, and assist trainees in exploring their attitudes regarding bullying/mobbing.

Coaching of HR personnel can play a critical role on the prevention of bullying/mobbing (Ferris, 2009). Consultants can assist HR personnel in developing and asserting their unit in preventing bullying/mobbing. Beyond coaching, consultants can assist HR personnel to develop programs and activities that are related to the development of a harmonious workplace. Even minor social events sponsored by HR personnel such as "meet and greet" and "employee appreciation" event can be significant initiatives in the prevention of bullying/mobbing.

Other training initiatives by consultants could include determining target groups for antibullying/mobbing training through conducting or collaborating with needs assessment, facilitating groups in crafting training/workshop materials to the specific groups targeted, and assisting with program evaluation (Fox & Stallworth, 2009).

Beyond working in partnership with HR personnel in coaching and sponsoring social events that foster cohesiveness, consultants can join forces with consultees in prevention efforts through being involved in employee selection, performance management, and development of reward systems (Ferris, 2009). In one example, a consultant pooled resources with a group of managers with hiring responsibilities to develop a screening process designed to select employees for hiring who scored high on an integrity component of an assessment. In another example, consultants worked together with managers in developing team-based versus individual-based performance rewards.

Consultation at the Organizational Level. One role that consultants with a preventive perspective can take on at the organizational level is conducting or collaborating with personnel in diagnosing the organization's orientation toward bullying (Ferris, 2009). The results of the diagnosis provide a guide for implementing preventive interventions. There are three popular frameworks for assessing the organization's orientation (Ferris, 2009). These include how an organization is prepared to respond to allegations of bullying/mobbing, the process model, and the Rayner and McIvor Typology (Rayner & McIvor, 2006, cited in Ferris, 2009).

Organizations can be prepared to respond to allegations of bullying/mobbing in several ways. In a worst-case scenario, the organization sees nothing wrong with bullying/mobbing. In a middle-case scenario, the organization doesn't directly promote bullying/mobbing but typically views workplace aggression as a function of the personalities of the parties involved. The best-case scenario is when the organization sees bullying/mobbing as destructive and is proactive in dealing with incidences and in prevention.

The process model (Salin, 2003, cited in Ferris, 2009) suggests that there are organizational processes (and structures) that promote bullying/mobbing: enabling, motivating, and precipitating. An example of an enabling process is weak leadership. A high level of competition within the organization is an example of motivating structures. Examples of precipitating processes that can promote bullying are changes in management and restructuring of work groups.

The Rayner and McIvor Typology (Rayner & McIvor, 2006; cited in Ferris, 2009) is a framework that ranks the effectiveness of an organization in dealing with bullying/mobbing on a 4-point continuum ranging from "oblivious" to "fragmented" to "near" to "strategic." Organizations at the "oblivious" end of the continuum have no plan for managing/preventing bullying/mobbing. "Fragmented" organizations have a passive (reactive) approach to managing/preventing bullying. The "near" part of the continuum suggests an organization that has an active approach toward managing/preventing bullying/mobbing yet accepts their occurrence. A "strategic" organization takes a proactive approach toward managing and preventing abuse.

No matter what framework consultants use, they can effectively take on a variety of roles in the management and prevention of bullying/mobbing by assisting organizations in fact-finding and diagnosing an organization's orientation toward bullying/mobbing. Consultants have a large number of interventions, such as team building and facilitating the development of antibullying policies, that can be used to prevent bullying/mobbing no matter what the outcomes of organizational diagnosis are (see Ferris, 2009). Even when organizational diagnosis indicates the presence of bullying/mobbing or enabling structures or processes for such, consultants can assist in prevention through a variety of interventions.

Consultants can, for example, conduct anonymous surveys and/or interviews that assess the perceived degree of workplace bullying/mobbing (Ferris, 2009). Consultants can facilitate a discussion of the results of the survey with decision makers, thus allowing them to develop new organizational strategies leading to the eradication of any bullying/mobbing.

One major intervention that is of particular interest to consultants with a preventive orientation is raising the organization's awareness of the issue of bullying/mobbing. Even if an organizational diagnosis does not show the presence of bullying/mobbing, consultants can decrease the probability of their future occurrence by promoting a better understanding of potential risks on the part of the members of the organization. Consultant interventions related to prevention include presenting case illustrations, definitions and descriptions of bullying/mobbing, and their costs to organizations that exhibit them to upper management through meetings or workshops (Ferris, 2009).

Policy development is another area in which consultants can assist in prevention (Duffy, 2009; Ferris, 2009). When organizations have a policy in place that specifically and explicitly deals with that particular organization's position on bullying/mobbing and related consequences, then that policy can positively affect prevention. From a prevention perspective, policy development can have the added positive consequence of influencing positive change in the organization's culture and foster positive work relationships among employees (Duffy, 2009). For policies to have the maximum preventive effect, they will need to have incorporated within them an effective procedure for policy enforcement (Namie & Namie, 2009) and for nurturing a positive work environment (Duffy, 2009).

Consultants can not only directly or indirectly effect policy development but also can affect the development of enforcement strategies, thus creating an even more powerful prevention effect. In one example, a consultant assisted an organization to develop a strong antibullying/mobbing policy that contained a statement of opposition to bullying/mobbing, a rationale for having such a policy, a statement of the importance of moving toward positive conduct, a definition of bullying/mobbing, examples of misconduct, antiretaliation clause, and a statement of rights of managers regarding the policy and its enforcement. Based on the consultant's recommendations, some important elements of enforcement procedures, including informal and formal complaint processes, a pledge of confidentiality, and the consequences of bullying/mobbing, were added (Namie & Namie, 2009). Activities for consultants after policy implementation include assessment of the effectiveness of the policy and input on the production of materials related to the policy implementation (Namie & Namie, 2009).

OD, with its emphasis on the entire organization, can assist in bullying/mobbing prevention. By focusing on culture change, consultants can help organizations prevent bullying/mobbing through strengthening areas of the organization such as reporting relationships, clarity of roles, and performance expectations (Namie & Namie, 2009).

Consultants can foster a preventive effect by working with organizations to develop a systematic conflict management approach that includes a preventive as well as a remedial aspect (Fox & Stallworth, 2009). For example, the conflict management system could have procedures for mediation in place for settling minor disputes before they turn into full-blown cases of bullying/mobbing.

The final area for consultants to have a preventive effect with organizations in the area of bullying/mobbing is providing consultation to enhance the organization's ability to be a "high-care" (Duffy, 2009, p. 249) organization. High-care organizations have caring as a core value, which is more nurtured than managed by leaders. There are basic consultant strategies to assist an organization in increasing its caring nature. These include increasing morale and changing the organization's culture to a more positive orientation through working with its leaders to develop appropriate strategies such as increasing informal events (e.g., Employee Appreciation Day) and including positive culture as a part of the organization's strategic plan. Through consultative activities such as increasing the organization's focus on people and on a positive, caring, and nurturing work environment, consultants can influence an organization's capacity not only to prevent mobbing/bullying but also to prevent other negative workplace issues.

Case Study Example

Chris, a mental health professional with vast experience in organizational consultation, has been asked by an organization to assist in assessing its vulnerability to workplace bullying/mobbing and in making related recommendations. Chris first meets with upper-level management to explore what they are looking for and clarify their perceptions regarding the organization's state of affairs related to bullying/mobbing. Chris then provides an outsider's perspective after a preliminary exploration of the issues is completed. In a follow-up meeting with the same group, Chris and the group together outline suggestions for proceeding. Chris and the group agree on the nature of the consultation, and a contract is developed accordingly. The consultation contract specifies that the consultant, in unison with selected members of the organization, will engage in the following activities while emphasizing the collaborative role whenever appropriate:

- Conduct or facilitate, as necessary, a diagnosis of the organization's orientation toward bullying/mobbing
- Facilitate the selection of interventions for raising the organization's awareness of issues related to bullying/mobbing
- Engage selected members of the organization in a review of current organizational policies to determine if there is adequate coverage related to bullying/mobbing management and prevention
- Assist the organization in assessing broader variables within the organization's culture such as morale, role clarity, and informal events that might be related to bullying/mobbing prevention

In diagnosing the organization's orientation toward bullying/mobbing, Chris and some members of the organization's HR unit used both surveys and interviews. A sampling from all segments of the organization was gathered. Prior to the data-gathering process, the chief executive officer (CEO) of the organization and each upper-level manager communicated about the organization's engagement with the consultant and what those activities entailed and provided encouragement to accept and cooperate with the consultant. Chris and the HR personnel also examined the formal policies and procedures of the organization that might be related to bullying/mobbing and organizational climate in general.

After analyzing the data from the interviews, surveys, and organizational records, Chris wrote a report of the findings. The HR department then reviewed the report and made additional suggestions for Chris to incorporate. The report was then shared with the original upper-level management group in an afternoon retreat. Chris and the HR personnel had used the Rayner and McIvor typology mentioned above and had diagnosed the organization as "fragmented" in its approach to bullying/mobbing. The "good news" was that the organization had minimal incidences of bullying/mobbing, and their occurrence was not seen as a major issue throughout the organization. The "bad news" was that some employees at the lower end of the organization reported that they had seen some incidences of bullying in the recent past, and awareness of the nature of bullying/mobbing was quite low throughout all levels of the organization. Additional negatives about the organization included the fact that there was not a clear policy on bullying/mobbing and that there were issues in the organizational climate that could foster bullying/mobbing. Thus, the organization was quite vulnerable to any forces, internal or external to the organization, which fostered bullying/mobbing.

Based on the discussion of the report at the workshop, Chris facilitated the upper-management team in a planning session designed to assist the organization in better dealing with any incidences of bullying and to develop measures for preventing the occurrence of bullying/mobbing. Chris used the nominal group technique (Delbecq, Van De Ven, & Gustafson, 1975) to help the group determine the facilitating forces and restraining forces for each of the recommendations. If the restraining forces too heavily outweighed the facilitating forces, the intervention was eliminated from further consideration. For example, if the overall cost of a prevention program outweighed the predicted reduction in bullying and the effect of fostering a more positive working climate, then that prevention program was further considered. Otherwise, the other recommendations were worked on in terms of maximizing the facilitating forces operating on them and minimizing related retraining forces. Following this process, the group, under the consultant's facilitation, prioritized the interventions.

The results of this process led to acceptance of and a strategy for each of the following recommendations, all of which were to have significant consultant involvement but with an emphasis on building the capacity of the members of the organization who were involved in the consultation to manage similar situations in the future:

- Facilitate the organization's HR unit in developing and implementing a bullying/mobbing awareness and prevention campaign aimed at all employees.
- Assist the organization's HR unit in a minor restructuring of the unit so that there was designated responsibility within that unit of ensuring a proactive and systematic approach at the organization level for managing and preventing bullying/mobbing.
- Train HR personnel in conflict resolution training for use in employee conflicts that may lead to bullying/mobbing if not preempted.
- Lead the top management team in the development of bullying/mobbing policy that has stated consequences for violations.
- Review all pertinent materials and activities to ensure that they involve preventive as well as remedial aspects.
- Conduct an additional needs assessment related to the climate of the organization and make related recommendations for increasing climate-enhancing opportunities such as informal events at work, increased use of teams, and streamlined communication processes within the organization that could prevent bullying/mobbing.

Over the next 6 months, Chris worked with the members of the organization to implement the recommendations and related strategies. Recent turnover in the HR leadership allowed Chris to move quickly in collaborating with HR personnel in developing the awareness and prevention campaign as well as assist the CEO to restructure the HR department. Campaign materials were developed in unison with a task force from all levels of the organization. Based on task force input, the materials developed were unique to the organization with prepackaged materials and programs being excluded. All materials included preventive as well as remedial elements and activities. The new head of the HR department was designated as the person responsible for ensuring a proactive and systematic program for dealing with and preventing bullying/mobbing, including the lead for implementing the campaign. The CEO ensured that all upper-level management people were provided opportunities for ongoing input about the campaign's progress and the organization's developing approach for dealing with and preventing bullying/mobbing.

The CEO worked very closely with Chris and a small group of employees from throughout the organization in determining the best ways to assess the needs of the organization in terms of making it even more "people friendly." The CEO was particularly concerned about overdifferentiation of departments within the organization. This had led, in the CEO's opinion, to a "the-left-hand-doesn't-know-what-the-right-hand-is-doing" type of mentality, with internal communication within the organization suffering. Chris and the aforementioned group developed a survey that addressed this as well as other concerns expressed by the CEO and others who had been interviewed during the consultation process. The results of the survey validated the CEO's concerns. Chris and the group recommended two interventions. First, all top-level managers were instructed to conduct weekly "town hall" meetings for their units. These meetings involved presenting updates on the organization as a whole as well as on the particular unit. In addition, attendees were encouraged to ask questions and bring up issues of concern for them. On another recommendation, the CEO set up a quarterly meeting open to the entire organization in which top management updated the employees regarding events in their particular department and solicited employee questions and input.

The new leader in HR was very amenable to having Chris use a "train-the-trainer" approach to preparing the HR unit to be more proactive in dealing with incidences of bullying/mobbing and their prevention. The HR director believed that such an approach would prepare personnel in being able to conduct effective training in the future without resorting to external consultants, thus increasing the preventive capacity within the organization. Chris trained the group in conflict resolution and mediation. During the training, Chris recommended that these interventions be done with issues between or among employees that were thought serious enough to lead to bullying or mobbing if they weren't resolved. Training in interventions for incidences of bullying/mobbing that had already occurred included policy implementation procedures and remedial actions, such as coaching. Chris also trained top-level management in these interventions, while HR personnel conducted training down to the supervisor level.

Representatives from several areas of the organization were involved in the development of the formal policy concerning bullying/mobbing. Chris brought in samples of policies from other organizations as a way to both educate about the nature of such policies and stimulate the thinking of top management in developing a policy specific to the organization. Chris then collaborated with a group in the development of the specifics of the policy. Consequences for bullying/mobbing were spelled out. The group then developed a special section within the policy that aimed at the creation and maintenance of a positive work environment that fostered good will among all employees.

During this process, it became increasingly clear to both Chris and the CEO that the CEO needed to add the role of being a "cheerleader" regarding bullying/mobbing prevention in particular and for enhancing the positive climate of the organization in general. To these ends, the CEO started to do more managing by walking around and holding "town meetings" designed to update employees to events effecting the organization as well as noting the importance to the organization and its employees of everyone getting along and working together. The CEO also started to send monthly e-mails out to employees who championed strong team work and camaraderie among the organization's members.

In a follow-up consultation 6 months later, Chris conducted a series of surveys and interviews regarding bullying/mobbing with selected organization personnel from all levels of the organization. Chris did this without assistance only to ensure that the follow-up information was as free from internal bias as possible. The results indicated a significant increase in the awareness among employees of the bullying/mobbing policy and its contents. Not only that, but a significant number of the employees were aware of the bullying/prevention program. The organizational climate had become even more positive, and employees reported liking the increased opportunities for informal involvement. For example, there was a great deal of praise for the newly formed clubs such as the road cycling team, the mountain biking team, and the creation of "Super Saturdays" during which employees and their families were invited to a company-sponsored event that provided lunch along with games and other enjoyable social activities. Survey and interview results suggested that the CEO's messages were getting through to the employees. As one respondent noted, the CEO was seen as a "real human being, one of us." Another important finding was that employees viewed bullying/mobbing as very unlikely occurrences in the organization, and the recent changes in the organization were most likely to continue to prevent their occurrence. Chris agreed to conduct a detailed follow-up assessment regarding bullying/mobbing and their prevention in the organization in 1 year and another 2 years out. The goal of the organization was to be rated "strategic" in terms of responding to bullying/mobbing and their prevention.

Learning Exercise 5

"Presentation Time!"

You are a mental health professional who has been contracted by *Hit The Fan Enterprises* to do consultation on workplace bullying/mobbing. In the spaces below, outline five of the basic ideas you would want to get across to attendees about preventing workplace bullying/mobbing.

_____

_____

_____

_____

_____

_____

Illustrative Example 2: Consultation in Bullying and Mobbing Prevention in Schools

Bullying is an important issue in schools. Much of the literature on school bullying tends to consider bullying and mobbing as synonymous. Therefore, in this section I refer to both of these phenomena under the rubric of "bullying." Media coverage of school bullying has been such that most people in our society are well aware of it. Whereas workplace bullying typically involves adults as perpetrators as well as victims, bullying in schools is most often characterized as student-to-student aggression. A further distinction is that definitions of workplace bullying/mobbing typically do not include physical violence, whereas physical violence can be part of bullying by students at school. Bullying is so extensive in the United States that the U.S. government has developed a website, http://stopbullyingnow.hrsa.gov, to deal with bullying and its prevention. Sections of this website include information on bullying prevention materials and programs.

What constitutes bullying from a school perspective? Following along the lines of Olweus (1994), Felix and Furlong (2008) define bullying as "aggressive behavior involving intentional infliction of harm on another person in a relationship characterized by an imbalance of power" (p. 1279). These authors note that bullying can involve physical and/or verbal aggression. Bullying can also involve the use of gestures. This form of bullying is called nonverbal bullying. The target of bullying may also include the victim's relationships as well as their physical well-being. There is a more subtle form of bullying in which victims are isolated from normal school social groups. This is often called emotional bullying. A newer form of bullying is cyberbullying. Cyberbullying is "an aggressive, intentional act carried out by a group or individual, using electronic forms of contact, repeatedly and over time against a victim who cannot easily defend him or herself" (Smith et al., 2008, p. 376).

Cyberbullying can be done through e-mails, instant messaging, web pages, blogs, and other forms of electronic communication.

No matter what form it takes, bullying is typically repetitive with the same individual or group bullying the same victim. Incidences of bullying in schools are pervasive and affect all levels of schooling. Most students will experience bullying during their time in school (Felix & Furlong, 2008). Some students are more bullied than others. That said, it is difficult to assess the psychological damage that even one experience of being bullied can have. In their review of the literature, Felix and Furlong (2008) found that there are many deleterious effects of victims of bullying. These include lower self-esteem, withdrawal from social activities, increased mental health issues, and school avoidance.

Conceptualizations of the causes of bullying in schools parallel those in the workplace. As in the workplace, bullying in schools is a complex phenomenon. Conceptualizations include characteristics of the individual, family, peer group, classroom, and the school (Orpinas & Horne, 2006; Swearer & Espelage, 2004). Each of these conceptualizations includes both risk factors and protective factors. Risk factors are attributes/conditions that promote bullying, whereas protective factors inhibit or prevent bullying (Orpinas & Horne, 2006).

The examination of the individual characteristics of a bully is one way to look at bullying and its causes. Research has identified three types of school bullies: the aggressive bully, the follower bully, and the relational bully (Orpinas & Horne, 2006). Aggressive bullies are proactive in using overt aggression. Followers, often called passive bullies, may start the bullying process but yield to the aggressive bully in carrying the process out. Relational bullies use subtle and covert methods, like isolating an individual from the peer group, to bully.

Family risk and protective factors are important elements in school bullying (Orpinas & Horne, 2006). Risk factors include basic parental practices, the amount of existing violence in the family system, and the degree of child neglect. Protective factors include the broad concept of high quality parenting. The concept breaks out to include "loving parents who spend time and energy in parenting" (Orpinas & Horne, 2006, p. 46). In this type of family setting, high expectations are held for children, communication among family members is strong, parental involvement in children's interests is high, and common family rituals exist.

The peer group to which a student belongs can influence whether or not that student engages in bullying (Swearer & Espelage, 2004). Bullies tend to be liked by other aggressive children but disliked by many nonaggressive children. Peer factors–related bullying include status within the peer group, time spent in social contact with peers, and time spent alone. Protective factors including parental support and love help children choose peer groups that engage in constructive and positive behaviors.

The climate of a given classroom, often dictated in large part by the teacher's attitude about bullying, can be a determiner of bullying (Swearer & Espelage, 2004). The teacher's lack of classroom management skills, poor teaching skill sets, low academic and behavior expectations for students, and poor teacher–student relationships all can promote bullying.

Characteristics of the school itself, such as school climate, can foster or prevent the occurrence of bullying (Orpinas & Horne, 2006; Swearer & Espelage, 2004). The schools' discipline plan, the degree and type of adult supervision, and the amount of aggressive behavior by adults at school are all factors related to bullying. Protective factors include teachers who engage students in learning, a caring school climate, and a specific policy on bullying.

Bullying can be conceptualized as being fostered or prevented by the social ecology of a given school. The occurrence as well as the prevention of bullying is a complex interplay among the "relationships between the individual, family, peer group, community, and culture" (Swearer & Espelage, 2004, p. 3). Because people are affected by their environment, efforts to reduce the incidence of or prevent bullying should take the nature of the environment into consideration. According to ecological theory, every school is unique. As a result, efforts at prevention, including consultation, need to be contextualized to the characteristics of the school, while also aiming at implementing empirically validated programs.

The Role of the Consultant in the Prevention of School Bullying

As with bullying prevention in the workplace, consultants can be a powerful force along with stakeholders making a variety of interventions at all levels of the organization. To better illustrate the impact of the preventive effect of consultation on the social context of the school, this section is organized from the perspective of the areas of school life that could benefit from consultation. As with many types of consultation, the preventive effect can be even more beneficial in the long term when the consultant takes on the collaborative role with consultees whenever feasible. Consultees, when heavily engaged in the consultation process, may well enhance their capacity to manage similar situations in the future more readily.

Consultants can assist with prevention program selection, conducting needs assessment about bullying, and helping in data-based selection of programs. Furthermore, consultants can engage in preventive activities by educating and training school staff and parents about what we know about bullying in schools.

Consultants, in education training activities such as workshops or other professional development activities, can assist school personnel in becoming aware of the nature of bullies and victims, the types of bullying, and the consequences of bullying. In addition, consultants can help school-based professionals understand the risk factors related to becoming a bully or victim. As important and from a preventive perspective, consultants can make school personnel aware of protective factors related to bullying, for example, commitment to learning, positive values related to conflict resolution, social competence skills such as problem-solving and social relationships skills, and positive identity factors such as enhanced self-esteem (Orpinas & Horne, 2006).

Consultants can provide information of the relationships between peer groups involvement and bullying in terms of the peer group characteristics of bullies and methods for redirecting children at risk for bullying into different and constructive peer group activities. Consultants can also point to the importance of parent behavior in determining the type of peer groups their children will select.

Similarly, consulting in the collaborative role with schools can change the climate to increase the protective factors related to bullying while decreasing risk factors. For example, school-based consultants serve on a team with a school's administration and faculty to develop and implement a detailed antibullying plan.

Although school personnel recognize bullying and typically understand its components, they are often unaware of theoretical perspectives of bullying and its prevention. Consequently, consultants can provide a variety of perspectives related to bullying and its causes. In one example, a consultant provides professional development to school staff on the social cognitive theory related to bullying and how staff can assist students to have increased self-efficacy related to managing conflict through role-playing activities.

If one assumes that a positive school climate and student social competence are integral to preventing bullying in schools, then consultants along with school personnel have a vast number of possible interventions to employ. Regarding school climate, for example, consultants can partner with school stakeholders in a variety of interventions related to enhancing the many components of a school's climate:

- Excellence in teaching
- School values
- Awareness of strengths and problems
- Policies and accountability
- Caring and respect
- Positive expectations
- Support for teachers physical environment (Orpinas & Horne, 2006)

Excellence in teaching really translates to high student academic performance, and a positive classroom climate is related to high academic achievement. Consultants, for example, could assist administrators in a school, or better yet, an entire school district, to develop a beginning teacher support program that not only includes best practices for instruction but also integrates best practices in developing positive social behaviors in students, thus having a preventive effect on the occurrence of bullying.

The values esteemed by a school and the degree to which those values are integrated into the everyday school life can have a strong preventive effect on bullying (Orpinas & Horne, 2006). Consultants can assist in this process by participating in activities designed to identify their core values, getting those values accepted by constituents within the school's ecology, and developing policies and procedures that reflect those values.

In this era of accountability, one would think that most schools would have a good grasp on their strengths and weaknesses. While that may be somewhat true for academic achievement, many schools have yet to identify possible strengths and weaknesses. For example, the personnel in a school may have no clue about the amount or nature of bullying going on. Consultants can be a part of initiatives in the school that result in a better understanding of the degree of the occurrence of bullying as well as the attitudes and perceptions about bullying of each of the groups that make up the school community. In one example, a consultant conducts interviews and surveys, the results of which suggested a low incidence of bullying but little knowledge on the part of school groups about preventing bullying in the future. In another example, a consultant partners with a school psychologist and school counselor in assessing the attitudes about bullying of a school's stakeholder groups.

Clearly, the policies of a school or school district and the resultant accountability, or lack thereof, can be an important variable in bullying prevention. Consultation can strongly affect the prevention of bullying through service to school districts and their individual schools in developing antibullying polices. For example, a consultant teams with a school district to ensure that consequences for bullying are clearly spelled out and to add preventive districtwide strategies such as ensuring that administrators of individual schools annually disseminate the policies to all stakeholders and review the policy with staff and students.

As one might surmise, caring and respect in schools are more easily talked about than integrated into the school climate. That said, there are many activities by which consultation can promote a school climate that prevents bullying through an atmosphere of respect and caring. For example, consultation could lead to school administrators incorporating methods for modeling caring and respect by school staff in the school's handbook as well as providing administrators with activities for training school staff in specific behaviors related to caring and respect.

Even the best of well-intended teachers can be overwhelmed by being asked to add one more thing to their schedule such as making the prevention of bullying a priority. A consultant could participate with teachers in their departmental or grade-level meeting by including a small amount of training time on the agenda. The focus of the training could be a "train-the-trainer" model in which the teachers help the students they teach to learn behaviors related to the prevention of bullying. A main point for the consultant to make is that the investment of the time in learning bully prevention skills now will make the teacher's life at work easier in the future. In another example, a consultant partners with a departmental team that is focusing on building classroom spirit.

The school's physical environment is an integral part of school climate. Consultants can assist schools in developing a school crisis and safety plan that is designed to minimize all types of violence including bullying. In another example, consultants can aid administrators in the development of a school pride program that involves all the groups of the school community.

The enhancement of student social competence can be effective in the prevention of bullying (Orpinas & Horne, 2006). Consultation can result in school personnel determining a variety of ways to enhance student social competence. Increased social competence means more positive peer relationships and, hence, less bullying. In an expert role, consultants can conduct workshops on the elements of student social competence and the methodology for enhancing it. As will be shown below, consultants can also be involved with bullying prevention programs that focus on student social competence. In a collaborative role, a consultant could work in partnership with a group of teachers in developing empathy training for the school's sixth-grade students.

From an ecological perspective, consultants can assist schools in the selection, implementation, and evaluation of bullying prevention programs. It is one thing to have an evidence-based bullying prevention program but another to adapt that program to a specific school so that the integrity of the program is maintained, while the school context is taken into consideration. To that end, consultants can play an important role. Consultants, for example, can aid school staff in contextualizing an empirically validated program to the individual characteristics of a school and its community.

Furthermore, a consultant, taking on a variety of roles, could partner with a school with a bullying prevention program in the following ways:

- Selecting a program that is best designed to the type of school (e.g., urban high school)
- Working with school groups to implement the program
- Participating in and conducting focus groups to get school-specific information for adapting the program
- Performing formative assessment to ensure that the program stays on track
- Partnering in conducting summative evaluation to demonstrate program effectiveness
- Aid with leading workshops and subsequent follow-up session that help staff implement the program from their role/function (e.g., helping teachers integrate social competence training with academic material)

Clearly, consultation can be an effective service that can be provided to schools to assist them in all aspects of bullying prevention. Table 5.1 summarizes many such interventions. External consultants can often bring a great deal of technical expertise that can be used for things like program selection and collaborative expertise to maximize engagement of consultees in the process. Internal consultants such as school counselors and school psychologists can provide contextual expertise that leads to the increased prevention of bullying as well as collaborative expertise to ensure that all local stakeholders have important and significant involvement and ownership in preventive initiatives. No matter whether consultants are internal or external, it is very important for them to ensure that knowledge, skills, and attitudes of all stakeholders are incorporated into any activity or intervention so that preventive effects are maximized.

Case Study Example

Sam, an external consultant with previous experience as a school mental health professional, has been hired by a district's only elementary school to assist in the development, implementation, and evaluation of a bullying prevention program. The school district containing the school has directed all of its three schools to develop bullying prevention programs of the highest quality. Sam arranges a follow-up meeting with the school administrators and the School Improvement Team (SIT) to explore in detail role expectations for the consultant. The SIT team consisted of stakeholders such as administrators, teachers, parents, support staff, and students. In addition, Sam provides an outsider's view of what it typically takes to initiate a quality bullying prevention

Table 5.1   Selected Examples of Consultation Interventions Aimed at Bullying Prevention in Schools

Employing education/training activities such as workshops about the nature of bullying
Making school climate changes by identifying and dealing with risk factors such as poor student–teacher relationships and protective factors such as building school belongingness on the part of all school members
Diagnosing a school's level of risk relative to bullying and developing related recommendations
Identifying school strengths and weaknesses related to school climate and bullying prevention
Developing and implementing school antibullying policies and procedures
Implementing strategies for developing an atmosphere of caring and respect
Analyzing the school physical environment and examining ways to make it as safe as possible
Integrating social competence training with the academic curriculum
Selecting an antibullying program that is the best fit for the school's context
Performing formative and summative assessment of an antibullying program's effectiveness
Conducting focus groups from stakeholders to determine desirable components of antibullying program
Employing a collaborative approach to all consultative activities to maximize input and skill development of all involved in bullying prevention activities

program. Both Sam and the SIT team agree that Sam should take on whatever roles are necessary to meet the expectations of the contract while emphasizing a collaborative role whenever necessary. Based on this information gathered in the meeting, Sam develops a proposal that was subsequently accepted and a contract signed.

The contract stated that Sam would consult with school personnel by providing the following services:

- Partner with the SIT team in incorporating bullying prevention into its scope of work
- Provide two workshops on the nature of school bullying and related prevention strategies
- Engage in a collaborative role with the school counselor and the district's school psychologist to determine the degree of bullying at the school and other factors related to a positive school climate
- Aid the SIT team to develop a bullying prevention program based on existing evidence-based programs and the unique characteristics of the school
- Develop with SIT team input and approval an evaluation scheme that includes both formative and summative assessment
- Provide follow-up assistance for 2 years in improving the program as needed

In partnering with the SIT team to incorporate bullying prevention into the scope of its work, Sam facilitated the use of a creative problem-solving process. The problem-solving process involved identifying the problem, analyzing it, developing solutions, and implementing a solution. Sam ensured that the collaborative role was used throughout the process to maximize the preventive effect on group members. As a result of going through the process, they would be better prepared to engage in effective problem solving in the future. The results of the problem-solving process led to a permanent subgroup within the SIT team that was to be dedicated to bullying prevention. The group was to have rotating membership with staggered terms and representation from each stakeholder group. Once the subgroup was appointed, Sam worked with its members to draft a plan of action that defined how the subgroup would operate and support the bullying prevention program that was going to be developed. The group members with Sam's facilitation determined that they would gather data on the group's effectiveness and analyze the data in relation to the SIT team dealing with the bullying prevention program as in their scope of work. If it appeared that the SIT team should be involved, then the team would adopt the solution and determine additional criteria to ensure that the effectiveness of the decision was refined and institutionalized.

Sam, as is common with external consultants who want to promote the maximum preventative effect to their work, tried to ensure that the SIT team had the necessary knowledge/skill sets necessary in dealing with the nature of school bullying and related prevention strategies for the SIT team. As a result, Sam, using the collaborative role of consultation, involved the entire SIT team in designing workshops that would be of use to the school staff in developing a bullying prevention program. Rather than being the "expert," Sam worked with the SIT team members to become experts on selected aspects of bullying and building prevention programs. Individual members would then share their expertise with the entire SIT team. One major focus of the workshops developed by the SIT team members was to make the other SIT team members aware of the nature of bullying. A second topic was on bullying prevention. This topic covered ways to help a school be more positive and caring and dealt extensively with how to develop a positive school climate. After the presentations on these topics by the SIT team members, Sam, using the collaborative role, facilitated the entire SIT team in making a plan for incorporating the results of the diagnosis of the degree of bullying at the school and the school's climate into the overall bullying prevention plan. Plans were then made for how SIT team's members would provide additional informal workshops/presentations on bullying prevention and enhancing the positive nature of the school's climate to groups of the school's stakeholders.

In assessing the degree of bullying at the school and related preventive strategies as well as ascertaining the degree to which the school has a positive climate, Sam, the school counselor, and the school psychologist conducted a series of focus groups, individual interviews, and surveys. Questions included those related to the who, what, when, where, and how of any bullying at the school; the types of things and events at school that prevented bullying; and the degree to which the school had a positive climate. Focus groups were run with groups of students from each grade, teachers from each grade level, and parents at a Parent Teacher Organization (PTO) meeting. Surveys were sent to selected community members and all parents. Teachers and other school staff completed an online survey. Structured interviews were held with randomly selected parents, school staff, and students.

Sam, the school counselor, and the school psychologist compiled a report based on the results of the data gathering. Sam provided the technical assistance in writing the report. The results of the data gathering indicated the following:

- Students viewed bullying to be a small but constant problem at the school, whereas other stakeholders did not view bullying as a problem at all.
- Awareness of the nature of bullying was not widespread among the stakeholders, whereas they were quite aware of the strengths of the school.

- All stakeholders believed that a detailed antibullying prevention program would benefit the entire school in many ways, including enhancing the positive nature of the school's climate.

The report concluded with a section of recommendations that included the need for awareness on bullying among stakeholders, the importance of having a bullying prevention program in place, and the significance of having preventive interventions such as those related to strengthening the social competence of the school stakeholders, particularly students, and bolstering the school's social climate. Copies of the report were disseminated to all stakeholder groups for discussion in various venues such as student council, PTO, and faculty meetings. All stakeholder groups voted to recommend the finding of the report for implementation.

The report provided insight into the characteristics of the school to which evidence-based bullying prevention program could be adapted. Sam frequently made the SIT team aware of the importance of both implementing an evidence-based program with integrity and adapting that program to the school context. Sam also noted to the group that all stakeholders needed to be part of program in order to maximize its preventive impact.

Sam and the SIT team reviewed a number of bullying prevention programs. The pros and cons of each possible program were developed in light of the school's context. Based on the SIT team's recommendation, the school adopted a nationally known program that targeted the entire school. The program was systemic and allowed room for the context of the school to be incorporated. The evaluation data regarding the program showed that it was effective in reducing the occurrence of bullying and also in preventing it. The program had a wealth of materials, including teacher manuals, parent study guides, videos, publicity recommendations, and a set of evaluation guidelines. The program emphasized student social competence and school climate enhancement. The program had additional materials for making new students and staff aware of the program and a set of strategies for the administrators to maintain stakeholders' involvement in and commitment to the program.

As a first step in implementing the program, Sam and the school's SIT team developed a process for stakeholders at the school to determine the school's core values and develop related behaviors to exemplify those values. The school ended up adopting the following as its core values: respect, responsibility, accountability, and honesty. The SIT team developed checklists that could be used to measure them. Sam and the SIT team then went on to work with the school by providing expertise in implementing the program.

After the initial implementation of the program, Sam visited the school for 2 days every 6 months and provided ad hoc consultation on any issues with the program and conducted informal and formal assessments to ensure that the program was staying on track.

Learning Exercise 6

"Choose Your Program"

As you will note, there are a large number of prevention programs for preventing bullying at school. You have been asked by the administration of an elementary school to recommend a bullying prevention program. Below, list the most important school and program characteristics that you would use in selecting the program.

School characteristics:

_____

_____

_____

_____

_____

_____

Program characteristics:

_____

_____

_____

_____

_____

_____

6

Summary and Conclusions

Overcoming Barriers to Implementing Preventive Consultation

Several things need to be in place to effectively implement the preventive aspects of consultation. According to Love (2007), these include the following:

- Ensure strong skill acquisition on the part of consultees to ensure generalization of knowledge and skills.
- Make certain that consultees understand the rationale for matching interventions to behaviors.
- Educate parties-at-interest about the "purpose, efficacy, and preventive aspects of consultation" (p. 168).
- Increase research to evaluate the preventive aspects of consultation.

Barriers to Prevention

Some authors such as Meyers et al. (1993) and Parsons and Meyers (1984) point out that one barrier that may keep mental health consultation from reaching its preventive potential is its focus on the remediation of the weaknesses of consultees as opposed to the development of their assets. As a result, mental health consultants can continue to reconceptualize consultation from a remedial perspective to one that encourages consultees to enhance knowledge, skills, confidence, and objectivity. One could imagine a consultant working with a consultee in such a way that the focus was on enhancing the consultee's strengths while simultaneously focusing on the problem at hand.

Another way to remove barriers to the preventive effects of consultation is to reconsider determining when consultation, relative to other possible services, is in order. For example, consultation and collaboration are similar yet different services. In consultation, the consultee carries out the plan that is developed. In collaboration, one professional works with one or more others to carry out the plan (Caplan & Caplan, 1993; Dougherty, 2009b). When professionals such as school counselors and school psychologists are internal to the organization in which problem solving is to occur, they may be better off serving as fellow collaborators than consultants to enhance the preventive effects of problem solving. Collaboration allows for modeling of techniques that may lead to mutual professional development among the collaborators as they go through the problem-solving process (Meyers et al., 1993). In other words, consultation is just one approach to problem solving that can have preventive effects. In fact, mental health consultation was developed by Caplan as just one approach for promoting the mental health of the community and preventing mental health issues (Trickett, 1993).

Enhancing Prevention in Consultation

Preventive consultation can be a powerful tool for professionals to use in their work. I close by making some suggestions for enhancing the preventive impact of consultation.

It is important for psychologists, counselors, social workers, and other human service professionals to be adequately prepared in preventive consultation. University coursework needs to cover the knowledge, skills, and dispositions related to effective preventive consultation. I teach a graduate course in consultation. As part of the course requirements, students write a research paper that links consultation and prevention. In addition, I train the students in preventive interventions. Students also have a field experience component to fulfill. Whenever possible, I encourage them to use a preventive approach in attaining their consultation experience.

Professional helpers can also engage in professional development activities related to preventive consultation. Reading the latest relevant works and research adds a deeper and richer understanding of the preventive effects of consultation. By becoming involved in prevention programs, mental health/ human service professionals can obtain significant experience that leads to a better understanding of the issues and gratifications related to prevention. It is a relatively easy step to then start to use consultation skills while being a part of a prevention program.

Finally, practitioners should bear in mind that consultation can have a preventive effect on consultees even when it deals with a remedial issue. It is important to remember that by going through the consultation process, the consultee not only gets assistance with the problem at hand but should also be better prepared to deal with similar problems in the future. To that end, consultants can maximize the preventive effects of consultation by making its preventive effects more explicit during the consultation process itself. Simple questions like "How do you think you could use the kind of things we have done in here with situations in the future that are similar to this?" can allow consultees to focus on integrating their consultation experience with how to approach the future.

Consultants and Prevention: A Summary

Consultation is an indirect service provided by mental health/human service professionals. This service entails a consultant delivering direct service to a consultee who in terms provides direct service to a client system. That client system can be an individual, group, or an entire organization. The consultant provides indirect service to the client system through the intermediary of the consultee.

Consultation requires strong skill sets in communication, problem solving, professional behavior, and working with groups and organizations. Consultants implement these skills when they take a variety of roles during the consultation process. These roles typically are categorized along a continuum from directive to nondirective. As an example, the expert role is considered as very directive.

The process of consultation consists of entry, diagnosis, implementation, and disengagement. These stages are further broken down into phases that structure the consultation process. This model is dynamic in that the stages can frequently overlap depending on what occurs during consultation.

There are three basic types of consultation: (1) behavioral, (2) mental health, and (3) organizational. Behavioral consultation applies the principles of learning to the consultation process. Mental health consultation focuses on the psychological well-being of the parties involved. Organizational consultation focuses on enhancing the efficacy and effectiveness of an organization and its members. These models tend to be more alike than not and typically go through the stages mentioned above.

Like any other mental health/human services activity, consultation is not without its limitations. All things considered, it may not necessarily be the service of choice in a given situation. Furthermore, the research base in consultation is limited in scope and breadth. Its practice has far advanced its research base.

Although consultation can be a strong force in promoting prevention, consultation's remedial capacity has received the most attention in both practice and research. From a preventive perspective, consultation can be used to lower the incidence of mental problems in populations and promote mental health in those populations. One major link between prevention and consultation is embedded in the consultee's experience in consultation. It is assumed that by experiencing the consultation process, the consultee not only receives assistance with the problem at hand but also generalizes the lessons learned to new, similar cases in the future.

Prevention can be related to consultation in two ways. First, there are models of consultation that emphasize prevention. Second, consultation can be applied to prevention programs to enhance their effectiveness.

One consultation model that emphasizes prevention is consultee-centered consultation. This model can assist individual consultees or groups of consultees to improve their capacity to deal with current and future individual clients or to become more effective in implementing a program or leading an organization.

Consultation models that emphasize positive psychology can have powerful preventive effect. The focus on assets, strengths, and capacity building encourages the development of skill sets and attitudes that are oriented toward prevention.

Systemwide organizational consultation offers the greatest potential for prevention in that it will affect the entire organization as well as the organization's interacting subsystems. Attention can be paid to primary prevention and risk reduction for the entire organization, thus creating an environment that fosters prevention.

Other models of consultation, such as behavioral, can also have a preventive effect by having the consultant model effective problem-solving behaviors that the consultee is able to transfer to current and future similar situations.

Consultation can be effective in enhancing the effectiveness of prevention programs. As would be expected, consultation services can assist in the development, implementation, and evaluation of prevention programs. Interventions made by consultants can range from providing technical expertise to fact-finding and from providing education/training experiences to facilitating effective problem solving on the part of consultees.

Clearly, consultation can be an effective way to promote prevention. In fact, this service was originally developed with prevention, as well as remediation, in mind. That said, the preventive aspects of consultation have not nearly received enough attention such that they have not achieved an equal footing with consultation's remedial aspects.

For consultation to realize its preventive potential, several things need to happen. More research on the preventive aspects of consultation is sorely needed. Mental health/human service professionals will need increased training and professional development in the theory and practice of prevention in consultation. Finally, more advocacy for and promotion of prevention in consultation from professional organizations and their memberships will keep prevention in the forefront of those organization's agendas.

References _____

Adelman, H., & Taylor, L. (2009). Ending the marginalization of mental health in schools. In R. W. Christner & R. Mennuti (Eds.), *School-based mental health: A practitioner's guide to comparative practices* (pp. 25–55). New York, NY: Routledge.

Akin-Little, K. A., Little, S. G., & Delligatti, N. (2004). A preventive model of school consultation incorporating perspectives from positive psychology. *Psychology in the Schools, 41,* 155–162.

Albee, G. (1959). *Mental health manpower trends.* New York, NY: Basic Books.

Albee, G. (1980). A competency model must replace the deficit model. In L. Bond & J. Rosen (Eds.), *Competency and coping during adulthood* (pp. 75–104). Hanover, NH: University Press of New England.

Albee, G. (1982). Preventing psychopathology and promoting human potential. *American Psychologist, 37,* 1043–1050.

Albee, G. (1985). The argument for primary prevention. *Journal of Primary Prevention, 5,* 213–219.

Alpert, J. L. (1976). Conceptual bases of mental health consultation in the schools. *Professional Psychology, 7,* 619–626.

Armenakis, A. A., & Burdg, H. B. (1988). Consultation research: Contributions to practice and directions for improvement. *Journal of Management, 14,* 339–365.

Babinski, L., Knotek, S., & Rogers, D. L. (2004). Facilitating conceptual change in new teacher consultation groups. In N. M. Lambert, I. Hylander, & J. H. Sandoval (Eds.), *Consultee-centered consultation* (pp. 101–113). Mahwah, NJ: Lawrence Erlbaum.

Bandura, A. (1969). *Principles of behavior modification.* New York, NY: Holt, Rinehart & Winston.

Bandura, A. (1977). Self-efficacy: Toward a unifying theory of behavior change. *Psychological Review, 84,* 191–215.

Barbarasch, B., & Elias, M. J. (2009). Fostering social competence in schools. In R. W. Christner, R. B. Mennuti, & J. S. Whitaker (Eds.), *School-based mental health* (pp. 125–148). New York, NY: Routledge.

Bell, M. E., & Goodman, L. A. (2006). Seeking social justice for victims of intimate partner violence. In R. L. Toporek, L. H. Gerstein, N. A. Fouad, G. Roysircar, & T. Israel (Eds.), *Handbook for social justice in counseling psychology* (pp. 155–169). Thousand Oaks, CA: Sage.

Bergan, J. R. (1977). *Behavioral consultation.* Columbus, OH: Charles E. Merrill.

Bergan, J. R., & Kratochwill, T. R. (1990). *Behavioral consultation and therapy.* New York, NY: Plenum Press.

Blom-Hoffman, J., & Rose, G. S. (2007). Applying motivational interviewing to school-based consultation: A commentary on "Has consultation achieved its primary prevention potential?" *Journal of Educational and Psychological Consultation, 17,* 151–156.

Brehm, K., & Doll, B. (2009). Building resilience in schools. In R. W. Christner, R. B. Mennuti, & J. S. Whitaker (Eds.), *School-based mental health* (pp. 55–85). New York, NY: Routledge.

Caplan, G. (1961). *An approach to community mental health.* New York, NY: Grune & Stratton.

Caplan, G. (1964). *Principles of preventive psychiatry.* New York, NY: Basic Books.

Caplan, G. (1970). *The theory and practice of mental health consultation.* New York, NY: Basic Books.

Caplan, G. (1974). *Support systems and community mental health.* New York, NY: Behavioral Publications.

Caplan, G. (1993). Mental health consultation: Community mental health, and population-oriented psychiatry. In W. P. Erchul (Ed.), *Consultation in community, school, and organizational practice: Gerald Caplan's contributions to professional psychology* (pp. 41–55). Washington, DC: Taylor & Francis.

Caplan, G., & Caplan, R. B. (1993). *Mental health consultation and collaboration.* San Francisco, CA: Jossey-Bass.

Caplan, G., & Caplan, R. B. (1994). The need for quality control in primary prevention. *Journal of Primary Prevention, 15,* 15–29.

Caplan, G., Caplan, R. B., & Erchul, W. P. (1994). Caplanian mental health consultation: Historical background and current status. *Consulting Psychology Journal: Practice and Research, 46,* 2–12.

Caplan, G., Caplan, R. B., & Erchul, W. P. (2005). A contemporary view of mental health consultation: Comments on "Types of metal health consultation" by Gerald Caplan. *Journal of Educational and Psychological Consultation, 6,* 23–30.

Caplan, G., & Caplan-Moskovich, R. (2004). Recent advances in mental health consultation. In N. M. Lambert, I. Hylander, & J. H. Sandoval (Eds.), *Consultee-centered consultation* (pp. 21–35). Mahwah, NJ: Lawrence Erlbaum.

Christner, R. W., Mennuti, R. B., & Whitaker, J. S. (2009). An overview of school-based mental health practice. In R. W. Christner, R. B. Mennuti, & J. S. Whitaker (Eds.), *School-based mental health* (pp. 3–22). New York, NY: Routledge.

Compton, W. (2005). *An introduction to positive psychology.* Belmont, CA: Cengage Wadsworth.

Conyne, R. K. (2004). *Preventive counseling* (2nd ed.). New York, NY: Brunner-Routledge.

Davidson, M. M., Waldo, M., & Adams, E. M. (2006). Promoting social justice through preventive interventions in schools. In R. L. Toporek, L. H. Gerstein, N. A. Fouad, G. Roysircar, & T. Israel (Eds.), *Handbook for social justice in counseling psychology* (pp. 117–129). Thousand Oaks, CA: Sage.

Delbecq, A. L., Van De Ven, A. H., & Gustafson, D. H. (1975). *Group techniques for program planning: A guide to nominal group and Delphi processes.* Glenview, IL: Scott, Foresman.

Doll, B., & Cummings, J. A. (2008). Best practices in population-based school mental health services. In A. Thomas & J. Grimes (Eds.), *Best practices in school psychology V* (Vol. 4, pp. 1333–1347). Bethesda, MD: National Association of School Psychologists.

Dougherty, A. M. (2009a). *Casebook of psychological consultation and collaboration in school and community settings* (5th ed.). Belmont, CA: Brooks/Cole Cengage.

Dougherty, A. M. (2009b). *Psychological consultation and collaboration in school and community settings* (5th ed.). Belmont, CA: Brooks/Cole Cengage.

Duffy, M. (2009). Preventing workplace mobbing and bullying with effective organizational consultation, policies, and legislation. *Consulting Psychology Journal: Practice and Research, 61,* 242–262.

Erchul, W. P., Grissom, P. F., & Getty, K. C. (2008). Studying interpersonal influence within school consultation: Social power base and relational communications perspectives. In W. P. Erchul & S. M. Sheridan (Eds.), *Handbook of research in school consultation* (pp. 293–322). New York, NY: Lawrence Erlbaum.

Erchul, W. P., & Martens, B. K. (1997). *School consultation: Conceptual and empirical bases of practice.* New York, NY: Plenum Press.

Erchul, W. P., & Sheridan, S. M. (2008). Overview: The state of scientific research in school consultation. In W. P. Erchul & S. M. Sheridan (Eds.), *Handbook of research in school consultation* (pp. 3–12). New York, NY: Lawrence Erlbaum.

Farrell, A. F. (2009). Building schoolwide positive behavioral supports. In R. W. Christner, R. B. Mennuti, & J. S. Whitaker (Eds.), *School-based mental health* (pp. 87–124). New York, NY: Routledge.

Felix, E., & Furlong, M. (2008). Best practices in bullying prevention. In A. Thomas & J. Grimes (Eds.), *Best practices in school psychology V* (Vol. 4, pp. 1279–1289). Bethesda, MD: National Association of School Psychologists.

Ferris, P. A. (2009). The role of the consulting psychologist in the prevention, detection, and correction of bullying and mobbing in the workplace. *Consulting Psychology Journal: Practice and Research, 61,* 169–189.

Fox, S., & Stallworth, L. E. (2009). Building a framework for two internal organizational approaches to resolving and preventing workplace bullying: Alternative dispute resolution and training. *Consulting Psychology Journal: Practice and Research, 61,* 220–241.

Frank, J. L., & Kratochwill, T. R. (2008). School-based problem-solving consultation. In W. P. Erchul & S. M. Sheridan (Eds.), *Handbook of research in school consultation* (pp. 13–30). New York, NY: Lawrence Erlbaum.

Gallessich, J. (1983). *The profession and practice of consultation.* San Francisco, CA: Jossey-Bass.

Gongora, J. N. (2004). Using consultee-centered consultation in a network intervention with health providers. In N. M. Lambert, I. Hylander, & J. H. Sandoval (Eds.), *Consultee-centered consultation* (pp. 171–185). Mahwah, NJ: Lawrence Erlbaum.

Greenberg, M. T., Domitrovich, C. E., Gracyzk, P., & Zins, J. (2001). *A conceptual model of implementation for school-based preventive intervention: Implication for research, practice, and policy. Center for Mental Health Services.* Rockville, MD: Substance Abuse and Mental Health Services Administration.

Gutkin, T. B. (1993). Cognitive modeling: A means for achieving prevention in school-based consultation. *Journal of Educational and Psychological Consultation, 4,* 179–183.

Gutkin, T. B., & Curtis, M. J. (1999). School-based consultation theory and practice: The art and science of indirect science delivery. In C. R. Reynolds & T. B. Gutkin (Eds.), *The handbook of school psychology* (3rd ed., pp. 598–637). New York, NY: Wiley.

Hojnoski, R. L. (2007). Promising directions in school-based system level consultation: A commentary on "Has consultation achieved its primary prevention potential?" *Journal of Educational and Psychological Consultation, 17,* 157–163.

Horne, S. G., & Mathews, S. S. (2006). A social justice approach to international collaborative consultation. In R. L. Toporek, L. H. Gerstein, N. A. Fouad, G. Roysircar, & T. Israel (Eds.), *Handbook for social justice in counseling psychology* (pp. 388–405). Thousand Oaks, CA: Sage.

Hughes, J. N., Loyd, L., & Buss, M. (2008). Empirical and theoretical support for an updated model of mental health consultation for schools. In W. P. Erchul & S. M. Sheridan (Eds.), *Handbook of research in school consultation* (pp. 343–360). New York, NY: Lawrence Erlbaum.

Illback, R. J., & Pennington, M. A. (2008). Organization development and change in school settings. In W. P. Erchul & S. M. Sheridan (Eds.), *Handbook of research in school consultation* (pp. 225–245). New York, NY: Lawrence Erlbaum.

Ingraham, C. L. (2004). Multicultural consultee-centered consultation: Supporting consultees in the development of cultural competence. In N. M. Lambert, I. Hylander, & J. H. Sandoval (Eds.), *Consultee-centered consultation* (pp. 133–147). Mahwah, NJ: Lawrence Erlbaum.

Ingraham, C. L. (2008). Studying multicultural aspects of consultation. In W. P. Erchul & S. M. Sheridan (Eds.), *Handbook of research in school consultation* (pp. 269–291). New York, NY: Lawrence Erlbaum.

Kaufman, R. A. (1971). A possible integrative model for the systematic and measurable improvements of education. *American Psychologist, 26,* 250–256.

Kelly, J. G. (1993). Gerald Caplan's paradigm: Bridging psychotherapy and public health practice. In W. P. Erchul (Ed.), *Consultation in community, school, and organizational practice: Gerald Caplan's contributions to professional psychology* (pp. 76–85). Washington, DC: Taylor & Francis.

Knoff, H. M., & Batsche, G. M. (1993). A school reform process for at-risk students: Applying Caplan's organizational consultation principles to guide prevention, intervention, and home-school collaboration. In W. P. Erchul (Ed.), *Consultation in community, school, and organizational practice: Gerald Caplan's contributions to professional psychology* (pp. 123–147). Washington, DC: Taylor & Francis.

Knotek, S. E., Kaniuka, M., & Ellingsen, K. (2008). Mental health consultation and consultee-centered approaches. In W. P. Erchul & S. M. Sheridan (Eds.), *Handbook of research in school consultation* (pp. 127–145). New York, NY: Lawrence Erlbaum.

Kratochwill, T. R. (2007). Preparing psychologists for evidence-based school practice: Lessons learned and challenges ahead. *American Psychologist, 62,* 829–843.

Lambert, N. M. (2004). Consultee-centered consultation: An international perspective on goals, process, and theory. In N. M. Lambert, I. Hylander, & J. H. Sandoval (Eds.), *Consultee-centered consultation* (pp. 3–19). Mahwah, NJ: Lawrence Erlbaum.

Li, C., & Vazquez-Nuttall, E. (2009). School consultants as agents of social justice for multicultural children and families. *Journal of Educational and Psychological Consultation, 19,* 26–44.

Lippitt, G., & Lippitt, R. (1986). *The consulting process in action* (2nd ed.). La Jolla, CA: University Associates.

Lopez, E. C., & Nastasi, B. K. (2008). An integrative view of process/outcome research from selected models of consultation. In W. P. Erchul & S. M. Sheridan (Eds.), *Handbook of research in school consultation* (pp. 247–265). New York, NY: Lawrence Erlbaum.

Love, K. B. (2007). Close but no cigar (yet): A commentary on "Has consultation achieved its primary prevention potential?" *Journal of Educational and Psychological Consultation, 17,* 165–169.

Martens, B. K., & DiGennaro, F. D. (2008). Behavioral consultation. In W. P. Erchul & S. M. Sheridan (Eds.), *Handbook of research in school consultation* (pp. 147–170). New York, NY: Lawrence Erlbaum.

McWhirter, B. T., & McWhirter, E. H. (2006). Couples helping couples. In R. L. Toporek, L. H. Gerstein, N. A. Fouad, G. Roysircar, & T. Israel (Eds.), *Handbook for social justice in counseling psychology* (pp. 406–420). Thousand Oaks, CA: Sage.

Meade, C. J., Hamilton, M. K., & Yuen, R. K.-W. (1982). Consultation research: The time has come the walrus said. *Counseling Psychologist, 4,* 39–51.

Meichenbaum, D. (1977). *Cognitive-behavior modification: An integrative approach.* New York, NY: Plenum Press.

Meyers, J., Brent, D., Faherty, E., & Modafferi, C. (1993). Caplan's contributions to the practice of psychology in the schools. In W. P. Erchul (Ed.), *Consultation in community, school, and organizational practice: Gerald Caplan's contributions to professional psychology* (pp. 99–122). Washington, DC: Taylor & Francis.

Meyers, J., Meyers, A. B., & Grogg, K. (2004). Prevention through consultation: A model for future developments in the field of school psychology. *Journal of Educational and Psychological Consultation, 15,* 257–276.

Meyers, J., & Nastasi, B. K. (1999). Primary prevention in school settings. In T. B. Gutkin & C. R. Reynolds (Eds.), *The handbook of school psychology* (3rd ed., pp. 764–799). New York, NY: Wiley.

Meyers, J., Truscott, S. D., Meyers, A. B., Varjas, K., & Collins, A. S. (2008). Qualitative and mixed-methods designs in consultation research. In W. P. Erchul & S. M. Sheridan (Eds.), *Handbook of research in school consultation* (pp. 89–114). New York, NY: Lawrence Erlbaum.

Miller, W. R., & Rollnick, S. (2002). *Motivational interviewing: Preparing people to change.* New York, NY: Guildford Press.

Namie, G., & Namie, R. (2009). U.S. workplace bullying: Some basic considerations and consultation interventions. *Consulting Psychology Journal: Practice and Research, 61,* 202–219.

Nastasi, B. K., & Varjas, K. (2008). Best practices in developing exemplary mental health programs in schools. In A. Thomas & J. Grimes (Eds.), *Best practices in school psychology V* (Vol. 4, pp. 1349–1360). Bethesda, MD: National Association of School Psychologists.

Noell, G. H. (2008). Research examining the relationships among consultation process, treatment integrity, and outcomes. In W. P. Erchul & S. M. Sheridan (Eds.), *Handbook of research in school consultation* (pp. 323–341). New York, NY: Lawrence Erlbaum.

Olweus, D. (1994). Annotation: Bullying at school: Basic facts and effects of a school based intervention program. *Journal of Child Psychology and Psychiatry, 35,* 1171–1190.

Orpinas, P., & Horne, A. M. (2006). *Bullying prevention.* Washington, DC: American Psychological Association.

Parsons, R. D. (1996). *The skilled consultant.* Needham Heights, MA: Allyn & Bacon.

Parsons, R. D., & Myers, J. (1984). *Developing consultation skills.* San Francisco, CA: Jossey-Bass.

Rayner, C., & McIvor, K. (2006). *Report to the dignity at work project steering committee: Research findings.* Portsmouth, England: University of Portsmouth Business School.

Salin, D. (2003). *Workplace bullying among business professionals: Prevalence, organizational antecedents, gender differences.* Helsinki, Finland: Swedish School of Economics and Business Administration.

Sandoval, J. (2004a). Constructivism, consultee-centered consultation, and conceptual change. In N. M. Lambert, I. Hylander, & J. H. Sandoval (Eds.), *Consultee-centered consultation* (pp. 37–44). Mahwah, NJ: Lawrence Erlbaum.

Sandoval, J. (2004b). Evaluation issued and strategies in consultee-centered consultation. In N. M. Lambert, I. Hylander, & J. H. Sandoval (Eds.), *Consultee-centered consultation* (pp. 391–400). Mahwah, NJ: Lawrence Erlbaum.

Schein, E. H. (1988). *Process consultation: Its role in organization development* (Vol. 1). Reading, MA: Addison Wesley.

Schein, E. H. (2004). *Organizational culture and leadership.* San Francisco, CA: Jossey-Bass.

Schmidt, C. K., Hoffman, M. A., & Taylor, N. (2006). Social justice related to working with HIV/AIDS from a counseling health psychology perspective. In R. L. Toporek, L. H. Gerstein, N. A. Fouad, G. Roysircar, & T. Israel (Eds.), *Handbook for social justice in counseling psychology* (pp. 358–373). Thousand Oaks, CA: Sage.

Schulte, A. C. (2008). Measurement in school consultation research. In W. P. Erchul & S. M. Sheridan (Eds.), *Handbook of research in school consultation* (pp. 33–61). New York, NY: Lawrence Erlbaum.

Seligman, M. E. P., & Csikszentmihalyi, M. (2000). Positive psychology: An introduction. *American Psychologist, 55,* 5–14.

Sheridan, S. M., & Gutkin, T. B. (2000). The ecology of school psychology: Examining and changing our paradigm for the 21st century. *School Psychology Review, 29,* 485–502.

Sheridan, S. M., Welch, M., & Orme, S. F. (1996). Is consultation effective? A review of outcome research. *Remedial and Special Education, 17,* 341–354.

Smith, P. K., Mahdavi, J., Carvalho, M., Fisher, S., Russell, S., & Tippett, N. (2008). Cyberbullying: Its nature and impact in secondary school pupils. *Journal of Child Psychology and Psychiatry, 49,* 376–385.

Snow, D. L., & Swift, C. F. (1985). Consultation and education in community mental health: A historical analysis. *Journal of Primary Prevention, 6,* 3–30.

Sperry, L. (1996). Leadership dynamics: Character and character structure in executives. *Consulting Psychology Journal, 48,* 268–280.

Sperry, L. (2009a). Mobbing and bullying: The influence of individual, work group, and organizational dynamics on abusive workplace behavior. *Consulting Psychology Journal: Practice and Research, 61,* 190–201.

Sperry, L. (2009b). Workplace mobbing and bullying: A consulting psychology perspective and overview. *Consulting Psychology Journal: Practice and Research, 61,* 165–168.

Stoiber, K. C., & Vanderwood, M. L. (2008). Traditional assessment, consultation, and intervention practices: Urban school psychologist's use, importance, and competence ratings. *Journal of Educational and Psychological Consultation, 18,* 264–292.

Strein, W., & Koehler, J. (2008). Best practices in developing prevention strategies for school psychology practice. In A. Thomas & J. Grimes (Eds.), *Best practices in school psychology V* (Vol. 4, pp. 1309–1322). Bethesda, MD: National Association of School Psychologists.

Sugai, G., & Horner, R. H. (2008). What we know and need to know about preventing problem behavior in schools. *Exceptionality, 16,* 67–77.

Sugai, G., Horner, R. H., Dunlap, G., Hieneman, M., Lewis, T. J., Nelsen, C. M., . . . Ruef, M. (2000). Applying positive behavior support and functional behavioral assessment in schools. *Journal of Positive Behavior Interventions, 2,* 131–143.

Swearer, S. M., & Espelage, D. L. (2004). Introduction: A social-ecological framework of bullying among youth. In D. L. Espelage & S. M. Swearer (Eds.), *Bullying in American schools* (pp. 1–12). Mahwah, NJ: Lawrence Erlbaum.

Tanyu, M. (2007). Implementation of prevention programs: Lessons for future research and practice: A commentary on social and emotional learning: Promoting the development of all students, a chapter by Joseph E. Zins and Maurice J. Elias. *Journal of Educational and Psychological Consultation, 17,* 257–262.

Tilly, W. D. (2008). The evolution of school psychology to science-based practice: Problem solving and the three-tiered model. In A. Thomas, & J. Grimes (Eds.), *Best practices in school psychology* (5th ed., Vol. 5, pp. 17–35). Bethesda, MD: National Association of School Psychologists.

Trickett, E. J. (1993). Gerald Caplan and the unfinished business of community psychology: A comment. In W. P. Erchul (Ed.), *Consultation in community, school, and organizational practice: Gerald Caplan's contributions to professional psychology* (pp. 163–175). Washington, DC: Taylor & Francis.

Vera, E., Daly, B., Gonzales, R. E., Morgan, M., & Thakral, C. (2006). Prevention and outreach with underserved populations. In R. L. Toporek, L. H. Gerstein, N. A. Fouad, G. Roysircar, & T. Israel (Eds.), *Handbook for social justice in counseling psychology* (pp. 86–99). Thousand Oaks, CA: Sage.

Willems, E. P. (1974). Behavioral technology and behavioral ecology. *Journal of Applied Behavioral Analysis, 7,* 151–156.

Zapf, D., & Einarsen, S. (2003). Individual antecedents of bullying: Victims and perpetrators. In S. E. Einarsen, H. Hoel, D. S. Zapf, & C. L. Cooper (Eds.), *Bullying and emotional abuse in the workplace: International perspectives in research and practice* (pp. 165–184). London, England: Taylor & Francis.

Zins, J. E. (1995). Has consultation achieved its primary prevention potential? *Journal of Primary Prevention, 15,* 285–301.

Zins, J. E., & Elias, M. J. (2006). Social and emotional learning: Promoting the development of all students. *Journal of Educational and Psychological Consultation, 17,* 233–255.

Index_____

About the Author_____

A. Michael Dougherty (PhD, Indiana State University) is Professor Emeritus of Counseling and former Dean of the College of Education and Allied Professions at Western Carolina University (WCU) in Cullowhee, North Carolina. He served as dean from 1998 until his retirement in 2009. During his tenure as dean, WCU's teacher education programs were recipients of both the American Association of State Colleges and Universities Christa McAuliffe Award and the Association of Teacher Educators Distinguished Program in Teacher Education Award. Dougherty's research interests currently include interpersonal processes in consultation and collaboration as well as textbooks in consultation and collaboration. He is author of *Psychological Consultation and Collaboration in School and Community Settings* (6th ed., in press) and *A Casebook of Psychological Consultation and Collaboration in School and Community Settings* (6th ed., in press). Dougherty has consulted, taught courses, and made presentations in a variety of international settings, including Barbados, Colombia, Cypress, El Salvador, Germany, Great Britain, Guatemala, Honduras, Jamaica, and Jordan.

⑤SAGE research**methods**

The essential online tool for researchers from the world's leading methods publisher

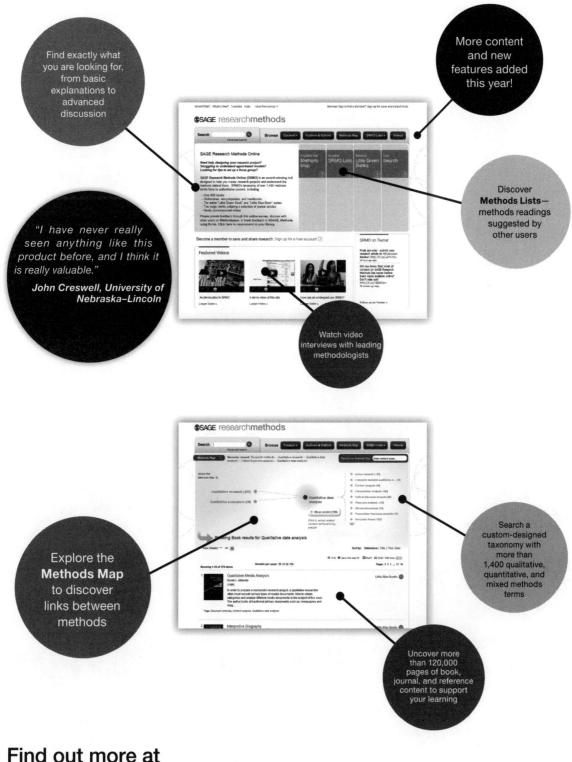

Find exactly what you are looking for, from basic explanations to advanced discussion

More content and new features added this year!

"I have never really seen anything like this product before, and I think it is really valuable."

John Creswell, University of Nebraska–Lincoln

Discover **Methods Lists**—methods readings suggested by other users

Watch video interviews with leading methodologists

Explore the **Methods Map** to discover links between methods

Search a custom-designed taxonomy with more than 1,400 qualitative, quantitative, and mixed methods terms

Uncover more than 120,000 pages of book, journal, and reference content to support your learning

Find out more at
www.sageresearchmethods.com